MW01277359

The Ecumenical
AFFAIR

LINDA VOGT TURNER

BALBOA.
PRESS

A DIVISION OF HAY HOUSE

Balboa Press books may be ordered through booksellers or by contacting:

Balboa Press
A Division of Hay House
1663 Liberty Drive
Bloomington, IN 47403
www.balboapress.com
1 (877) 407-4847

Print information available on the last page.

ISBN: 978-1-5043-3809-7 (sc)
ISBN: 978-1-5043-3810-3 (hc)
ISBN: 978-1-5043-3811-0 (e)

Library of Congress Control Number: 2015913229

Balboa Press rev. date: 09/10/2015

I dedicate this book to DonStewart, who listens
with his whole body and responds in love and faith,
believing *love makes the world go 'round!*

If I speak with the tongues of men and of angels, but do not have love, I have become a noisy gong or a clanging cymbal. If I have the gift of prophecy, and know all mysteries and all knowledge; and if I have all faith, so as to remove mountains, but do not have love, I am nothing. And if I give all my possessions to feed the poor, and if I surrender my body to be burned, but do not have love, it profits me nothing.

1 Corinthians 13:1-3 (New American Standard Bible)

Acknowledgements

This story was written in concert in part with Marguerite Duras' *The North China Lover: A Novel* and Robert Fulghum's *It Was on Fire When I Lay Down on It*. Duras' and Fulghum's creative nonfiction shaped mine.

My story could not have been written without the help, support and editorial services of Betsy Warland and Betsy Nuse. Ms. Warland is the co-founder of the Creative Nonfiction Collective, founder of The Writer's Studio at Simon Fraser University and director of the Vancouver Manuscript Intensive. Ms. Nuse has edited fiction and nonfiction for more than 30 years.

Toward the end of my undergraduate studies at Simon Fraser University (SFU), I enrolled in a feminist writing course led by Betsy Warland. I mistakenly thought it was merely a course where I would read the work of feminist writers. So did others enrolled in the class.

In the first class, Ms. Warland asked us, "How many of you are writers?"

None of us wanted to admit we were writers. Ms. Warland quickly set us straight. We were writers and most likely feminists because we had enrolled in her class. We had been writing essays for three and four years at least.

She then asked us, "Why do you write?"

Leaving us to think about that question, she proceeded to tell us we were indeed going to develop our writing skills in her class by reading the work of other feminists. We were then going to choose one author and use our own skills as writers to write in the style of our chosen author. I later chose to write in the style of Marguerite Duras.

Going home that night on the Sky Train, I thought about Ms. Warland's question, "Why do you write?" I realized I had been writing to ask the most important question of all. The one Robert Fulghum had asked the Greek: What is the meaning of life? So I sat down the next day on my sofa with Robert Fulghum's book, and *The Ecumenical Affair* began to take shape.

After the course ended I had a 25-page chapbook that I wrote and assembled with the help of Staples Canada Inc. However, I was not ready to think about writing more.

Eight years later, when by coincidence I answered a call to attend an eco-conference at the Orthodox Academy in Crete, I met Dr. Lucas Andrianos, who organized that conference. I was working at SFU in the School of Engineering Science as an administrator. I was also enrolled in SFU's Graduate Liberal Studies Programme. As a graduate student I was eligible to answer Dr. Andrianos' call. The call asked for an interfaith, interdisciplinary response to the environmental crisis facing the earth.

At the end of my presentation, Dr. Andrianos came up to me and mentioned he'd noticed I was from SFU. He then told me he had completed his postdoctoral studies there. And when I asked in what faculty, he replied The School of Engineering Science. We then figured out he'd left the school shortly before the school hired me and we had several colleagues in common. Lucas, his wife and children and I have become very close friends. Because of the true love I feel, both from and for, Lucas, his family, and the faithful connected with the Orthodox Academy of Crete, as well as that of the friends I have met there – Dean, Nora, Diana, and Lesya, I have gained the confidence to complete the writing of *The Ecumenical Affair*.

I am also very grateful for the love and support of my professors and friends at SFU over the years, and of course my friends at

Bethany-Newton United Church and all the people in the wider church who have prayed for me and encouraged me in large and small ways. Their love for living out the Gospel in community is a blessing and lifts me up, as does the work and prayers of people of other faiths who have made a point of connecting with me.

Lastly, I am truly grateful to singer, songwriter and actor DonStewart. He encourages me to write every day. More importantly, I am grateful for his love and faith in me and his profound knowledge of and faith in the Gospel. I am also grateful for the love of my children, my extended family, and DonStewart's family and friends. As DonStewart wrote on the signature quilt at Bethany-Newton's Inter-Ecothee Conference, "Love makes the world go 'round. Jump on!"

One

Vancouver
University of British Columbia
July 1983

A colossal tent sits in the middle of a wide expanse behind a grey, castellated structure. There on the lawn, with bold circus yellow-and-white stripes, everything is wide open. Like a revival meeting. There are strains of American spirituals, but also chants of "Veni, Sancte Spiritus" and "Kyrie Eleison" coming through the open flaps, beckoning people in suits, dresses and summer leisure.

The time is eight thirty. There are the fresh fragrances of dew and grass mingling with cedar shrubs and potted flowers. The faithful prepare for worship. Local television crews are setting up their cameras. The choir and the chancel focus our attention. Beautiful banners present a vista of mountains, sea and sky—light beams, and the letters *o i k o u m e n e* arch over a cross in a winged canoe. The shrubs and plants set off the front of a long table clothed in three blue and white foursquare banners. Rows of chairs on the grass wait to be filled. Thousands talking, listening. Hymns, prayers—each in a different language.

It is a revival meeting—lively, jubilant, festive.

Christians and robed, grey-bearded priests and bishops in black fill reserved chairs. They bear heavy iron crosses and sit apart from the rest.

Sitting with them is a middle-aged man, black hair, rugged good looks. Clean-shaven. He is the one who has no name in this story—the one called the Greek. He is Orthodox. He is not a priest.

The priest, the one the Greek is talking with, is a Roman Catholic and younger than the others. He is also Greek.

A woman joins them: short hair. Fair. Mature and confident. Beige summer skirt suit. That's Maria.

Following worship, a younger woman walks into a small lecture theater and takes her place facing those gathered to hear Maria speak. Microphones are set up in both aisles on the stairs halfway down. Maria looks around. There is a desktop lectern with a mike. She puts a folder on the lectern. Studies the faces in front of her.

Everyone has picture ID tags hanging from cords around their necks. The Young Woman doesn't have a picture ID. Pinned above her heart are the words "La Source, Daily Visitor Programme."

Someone takes Maria's picture. Two others rush forward to put tape recorders on the desk. Notebooks open, and writing desks flip up. People recline in soft, plush seats.

The Young Woman whispers to the man beside her. She can't flip up the writing desk. He shows her how.

Maria begins. She introduces herself as a Roman Catholic theologian, saying she has been asked to give a talk on God and gender. Maria says in her country people speak Portuguese and do not use gendered pronouns. God is not thought of as him or her.

The Young Woman listens to the Portuguese voice, each word carefully spoken. Sits in awe.

God is simply that entity who is ever-present with the person.

Maria notices the Young Woman, looks into her starry-bright morning eyes, and they steal her breath. God's Holy Spirit looks back.

She no longer remembers what she wants to say. Instead, she remembers the Young Woman standing alone in silence after the "Veni, Sancte Spiritus."

Maria looks down at her notes and returns her attention to the room. She remembers now. She wanted to say each human being is an animated body—an incarnate soul on which life depends. This life is a breath that comes from God. Creation and humans are in an everlasting relation with their Creator.[1]

People line up at the mikes. Not the Young Woman. She listens intently as questions and comments bounce back and forth from mike to mike to mike, her ponytail swishing from side to side.

3

Moralists argue that God created man in His own image first and instructed him to have dominion over the rest of creation. Then God created woman from man's rib—as man's helpmate. It is right for woman to submit to man's rule. Feminists disagree.

It is eleven thirty. The discussion is over. It's time to go for lunch at the Sub. The Young Woman does not know what or where the Sub is. She follows the crush. Everyone has a bleached cotton bag for books and papers. A blue and white silkscreened logo stretches across the front: *oikoumene*. This Greek word for ecumenism is clearly visible in white on blue, arching over a cross in a boat. Her straw bag cradles books and papers.

The Greek, in his shirtsleeves, slings a bleached cotton bag with the familiar blue logo over his shoulder. Looks at his watch. Lights a cigarette.

The Greek—older now. White hair. Sits on a terrace in the late afternoon sun. Gazes at the Aegean sea.

Abroad.

The Young Woman. Now middle-aged—now just the Woman— with short, cropped, tawny-brown hair, sits on a gold and green brocade sofa. On her lap is a best-seller she found at the church bookstore. Bold, parrot-green letters and a red circle on a gold mat atop a red leafy cover stare up at her.

IT WAS ON
FIRE WHEN I
LAY DOWN
ON IT

○

ROBERT
FULGHUM

She folds back the cover. Fans the pages. Stops. Creases it open—quarter way from the end.

"Are there any questions?" This question was asked by a Greek teacher, a philosopher and a legendary peacemaker ... after a two-week Socratic symposium on Greek culture.[2]

As participants rose to leave, Fulghum countered. "What is the meaning of life?"[3]

Hungry to know more, the Woman turns the pages, adding bits from what she already knows:

> The legendary philosopher is the general director of the academy dedicated to peace and reconciliation between Germans and Cretans who vowed they would never stop hating each other. The surrounding villagers are fishers, olive oil producers and yogurt makers. This village has a grave yard on top of a hill adjacent to the Academy. In these graves lay the bones of priests, nuns, farmers and fishers who dared to stop the invading Germans. The invaders were armed only with their side arms. The machine guns, ammunition and other weapons were air dropped in canisters. The invading soldiers were horrified to see nuns and priests, old people, and little children killing their comrades. On the

opposite shore—in Maleme—is the graveyard of the slain Germans.[4]

The Woman places the book on the cushion beside her. Open. Pages down. Rises. Goes over to the piano. Sees her face reflected in the mirror above the piano. Sees the backs of photos. Shifts her eyes forward to the gilded frames. Sees smiling faces. Blue eyes. Blond hair. German blood. Her children.

Returns to the sofa. Reads how the legendary philosopher, as a boy, found a mirror on the roadside belonging to a German motorcycle. It was broken into tiny bits. How he picked up the largest bit, smoothed her rough edges on a stone, played with her— shining the light she gleaned—into all sorts of places. How when he became an adult, he realized the meaning of his life was tied to that mirror.[5]

The Woman closes the bestseller. Stares at the bold, parrot-green letters and red circle on the gold mat atop the red, leafy cover. Face radiant. Blue eyes bright. Creases it open to the seventh unnumbered page: "Imagination is stronger than knowledge ... love is stronger than death." A mystery here.

Right hand under left elbow. Thumb under chin. Digits curled. First index digit rubbing her lips. Continues reading the author's note. Imagines: This story as a mirror on a fishing line ... with a bait and hook—to help her "show and tell."[6]

Turns to page three and imagines the newspaper story told there *is* the bait. A juicy tidbit of gossip. It's about a man rescued from a fire in an upstairs bedroom. When the fire responders ask, "How did it happen?" the Woman sees the Greek shrug, saying, "I don't know. It was on fire when I lay down on it."[7]

"And then a friend, adding his two bits: 'Why do you laugh? Change the name, and the story is told of you.'"[8]

Two

This is what the Woman says.

This is her story.
This is a passion play—a play about people
who are crazy-wise,
who speak their hearts,
who speak Greek.

The crew has doused the smouldering pallet.
How it happened matters.

On a tree-lined marine drive stately mansions and cars wind out to the University of British Columbia and its endowment lands.

This is Vancouver in July. The year is 1983.
This is the sixth assembly of the World Council of Churches.
The air is cool and trembling with heat.

The Woman is walking alone. She's carrying a straw bag. She looks like a student. She's dressed like one. Ponytail swishing back and forth. Bare feet in sunny yellow flip-flops. Wine-coloured toes. Slim. She is the one we saw earlier. The one with the words "La Source, Daily Visitor Programme" pinned above her heart who didn't know about the flip-top desk.

There are people everywhere; the joy, the laughter, the sounds of cutlery and crockery spill outside from inside—this must be the Sub.

Lines of people wait to enter. People are friendly. Class, race, gender barriers seem forgotten. People introduce themselves to strangers standing in line.

A place of communion.

Men in jackets. Some in shirtsleeves. Women in summer dresses. Some in skirts, others in pants, mingling with people in colourful caftans. Men wearing skullcaps. African women with stunning scarves twisted around their heads. Priests and nuns in long black robes. Students dressed for summer sprawl on the grass, talking. One girl has a tambourine. Two others dance, sing and clap.

bim Bom / bim bimbimBom / bim bimbimbim bim Bom/
shaBAT shaLOM (clap)/shaBAT shaLOM (clap)/
shabatshabat sha LOM (clap)

Waiting in line to eat, the Woman turns to the sound. A Hebrew folk song. For peace. She does not know this. The Greek is behind her. He asks how she spent the morning. She tells him about Maria's talk. Says she doesn't understand all the fuss over the issue of Man and Woman. Says: "It's simple. I am a man. I am a female man. I am a member of the race called man. You are a man. You are a male man. You too are a member of the race called man."

He grins.

She continues: "You—I suspect because you are here at this event—are a humanitarian. You help people. You are a helper, a helpmate of mankind."

His eyes light up.

She continues: "Therefore even though you're a male, you can be a woman."

His whole body bursts into a smile.

She quickly adds: "You are a male being, and you're a helpmate of Man. Therefore, if I—a female being—can belong to the race 'mankind' surely you, a male being, can belong to the race 'womankind.'"

Her eyes take in his maleness. Catches a glimpse of his undershirt beneath his white semi-transparent short-sleeved shirt before she turns and moves forward in the line.

He follows, his eyes taking in the curve of her hips in the tight parrot-green chinos buttoned at her tiny ankles. He asks: "What are you doing for dinner this evening?"

She picks up a tray and turns back toward him, smiling.

He continues: "Have you plans?" He leans forward, picks up a tray, places it on the grooved counter. Slides it forward, looking at her. "Will you grant me the pleasure of your company at dinner?"

Silence.

The Young Woman puts her tray in line. In front of his. Slides it forward. "I don't even know your name."

Turns back. Looks at his ID tag hanging from the cord around his neck. "Papa what?"

Laughs. Pronounces his name for her. Pushes his tray behind hers, asks: "Do you have a car? If you don't, can you rent one? I'll pay for it. … Tonight after dinner we could go for a drive and see the sights."

She places a garden salad on her tray. "What about after lunch?"

"No, I have to meet some people. I've got to prepare. I'm speaking in the plenary later."

Silence.

He asks: "Will you meet me here at six?"

"Yes."

"Can you get a car?"

"Yes."

Later that day in the Plenary.

The official delegates sit at long tables down on the floor facing saffron-draped tables. The blue logo visibly centered on a red carpeted stage. An immense red and yellow parachute-cloth banner hangs from the ceiling. Camera crews and translators are on hand. No one is allowed inside the building without proper ID. The accredited and daily visitors are upstairs in the bleachers. They wear headphones.

One grey-bearded man, sitting behind the Woman, sees her. She's listening. Watching intently as the lights dim, while from the shadows an icon is projected onto a movie size screen. The headset voice says:

"God is Love because God is Triune ... Andrei Rublev, the Russian Orthodox monk who painted it in 1422, intended it as an affirmation of Life ... icons are a kind of spiritual window between earth and heaven ..."[9]

At the break, the bearded man follows her outside. She asks him about the Greek. He says he doesn't know him. They don't go back in. They watch the plenary session on closed-circuit TV. They talk about Jungian psychology. She writes down some books that he recommends: *Man & His Symbols. The Feeling Child. The Primal Scream. The Sex Contract.*

He asks: "Why do you think you wear your hair long?"

"Because the Magdalene did."

"Are you worried about what could happen—if the Greek should come on to you?"

11

Blushing and fidgeting with her earring she says: "No."

Purses her lips. *Why should I worry? I'm the one with the car.*

He grins and tells her how he and others went skinny-dipping at Wreck Beach on the weekend.

She glimpses his wedding band.

So what if the Greek comes on to me? Why not enjoy the ride? Everyone is going to think I did anyhow. What would the Magdalene do? She kissed Jesus' feet, for Pete's sake. If Jesus is no sinner, neither is she, nor she who speaks with a he ... at noon or ... under the cover of darkness.

Six p.m.

The Greek is late.

When he arrives he apologizes and says he hopes it's okay. He's invited his roommate, Dimitri, to dine with them. He explains. Dimitri is a Roman Catholic father from the Vatican. They grew up together.

Dimitri asks her what she thinks about the protesters picketing yesterday outside the Student Union building.

She says: "They're evangelicals, fundamentalists. They take the Bible literally and are always trying to scare people about the end of the world, or the Antichrist. They say he's here at this assembly. What makes them so sure the Antichrist is a he? He could be a she."

Dimitri says: "I'm evangelical. I take Scripture literally. I believe the Scripture is the infallible Word of God. It's central and fundamental to my faith."

Undaunted, she continues to argue with Dimitri about the authority and interpretation of Scripture. She tells him how silly it is to think Moses actually heard God's voice speaking to him from a burning bush. "There are so many more possibilities. A bush can be a person, you know—a sage. Or a bush can line a gun chamber or be a pivot hole. So perhaps Moses saw an exciting loophole in the law, and this loophole let him speak with God in a new and exciting way."

Dimitri speaks—silences her. He's pleased. Jubilant. Looks right into the Greek's eyes and says: "Moses said he heard God speaking to him from a burning bush, and I believe him."

The Greek dressed for dinner. White shirt, black tie, olive-green suit. Pushes up his suit sleeves. Lights a cigarette.

He and Dimitri exchange words rapidly in Greek.

The word *anthropos* catches her attention.

On the way to the car the Greek says: "It will go bad for you if people see us together. Let's hurry."

At the car he says: "I need to stop and get a coat. Wait here. My room is up there." Points to an apartment tower.

He returns. As he closes the car door, she says: "It's my mom's. I borrowed it this week while my husband's away. He has ours. It's a Rally Sport."

"Sportster models are dangerous. Too racy. Dimitri mustn't see us leaving together. Go. That way."

The Woman drives along the marine drive winding its way out. Leaving the castellated structure behind.

The Greek says: "I've taken in all the tourist things. Stanley Park. Grouse Mountain. *SaLmon*"

His accent makes her smile.

"What kind of a doctor are you?"

"Of philosophy. I'm a gadfly."

"What's a gadfly."

"You know. Like Socrates. I go around stinging people out of their sleep."

He grabs her thigh, above the knee. Grips it hard. She feels the pressure of his hand. His desire. Removes it. Gives him a cool stare.

Silence.

He reaches into his breast pocket. Fishes for a cigarette. With his eyes he asks if she minds. Him smoking. He pushes up his suit sleeves. Lights a cigarette. Takes it from his mouth—cupping it between the third and fourth digits. With the hand that grabbed her. Pulls deeply on the first puff.

They talk about what they see.

He notices a sign that welcomes people to Delta.

She says: "As a letter it denotes the numeral four. As a triangle it symbolizes a perfect triune."

"It feels good to talk with someone who speaks Greek."

"The language of things not understood?"

Cigarette smoke fills the car. She doesn't actually speak Greek.

He nods. Inhales. Says: "The things ... between the lines." Exhales—pushing out his broad bottom lip with the smoke.

"At dinner. When Dimitri and you were talking. The only word I caught was anthropos. Were you telling him what I said at noon?"

He nods.

Silence. "Would you like to see where I live?"

The Woman's home.

A split-level house. Olive-green cedar. Oxford-brown trim. Two-car garage. Chocolate-bar doors. Grey shake roof. Edged lawn. Shrubs and bark mulch. Cement driveway, curbs and sidewalk. Underground wiring. Fenced side and backyards, trimmed to match the house. A blue and white swing set. On gravel. A play house, a patch of lawn, an umbrella clothes line. Cherry trees, hedges, more cement, river rock, a swimming pool. A diving board.

He asks about the neighbours.

She presses the button of the garage remote. She parks the dark-blue '78 Ford inside.

They wait until the door closes.

They go inside from the garage, through the laundry room, past the Woman's tiny office. Through the gold and copper family room, up into the kitchen, through the hall and into the living room. He stops to admire the mahogany Heintzman, notices a book open to Chopin's *Grande valse brillante in E-flat major, Op. 18*.

She goes to hang up his raincoat in the front hall.

Comes back.

He asks her if she is the one.

Who plays the piano and keeps the house?

She nods.

It is an elegant room. Gold sponge paint paper lines the walls. Sheer curtains with embroidered hems. Rich, dark-brown drapes and carpeting. A wide bay window and window seat. A gold and soft-green brocade sofa looks out the window, across the room, past the piano. The matching chair sits facing the room, facing the piano. Dark French Provincial tables. Brass table lamps. Few ornaments. Two armchairs with gold and green striped velvet cushions. A French Provincial dining room suite. Four side chairs match the ones in the living room. An etched mirror and pictures in gilded frames. On top of the piano—a boy and his little sister.

Silence.

She walks past him standing at the piano. He asks about her children. She says they are away with their father, camping. He asks why she didn't go. She says she wanted to take part in the Visitors Programme. She sits on the sofa in the middle. Invites him to sit.

He studies her face. Sits by the sofa arm. Rests his arm on the back of the sofa. She moves closer. He bends forward to smell her hair. Kisses her tawny bangs.

Night is falling. People are walking past the house with umbrellas. Through the folds of sheer, the lacy branch of the red maple, they can see. It's getting dark. The Woman gets up to turn on a lamp. She leaves the heavy drapes open. Returns to the sofa. He enfolds her under his arm. They continue for a moment watching and listening as the cars swish by.

The Woman asks: "In Greece ... are the men the head of the family?"

He laughs: "The women let us think so. But everyone knows women do this." He puts his hand on her head. Turns it toward him.

She looks directly into his eyes. She says: "It's no fun being a hand or a neck. If the head gets to tell them how to move."

"We men are such terrible beasts. We have egos."

She thinks: *And we women don't?*

He says nothing. Their eyes lock. She thinks: *No. Women … helpmates don't have egos, and that's what gives them power. Men must prove how strong they are. Real power is knowing who you are and how strong you are.*

She breaks away. They kiss.

"Tell me a story. About you. When you were a little boy."

He worms out of his jacket. Fishes into his shirt pocket for a cigarette. Cocks his left brow. She offers no resistance. He lights it. Grips it like before. Leans back. Puts his left foot up on his knee. Blows smoke away from her—pushing out his bottom lip. Continues: "When I was the age of the children in those pictures on the piano, the Nazis occupied my country. This you know?"

She shakes her head.

"When the parachutes came, villagers armed themselves with kitchen knives and garden scythes and hid in the long grass at the edge of the fields. As the paratroopers landed, the villagers attacked as many as they could. The German high command was of course outraged. In retaliation, they ordered the mass slaughter of whole villages: women, old people, children, babies. You've seen in movies how they do this?"

She nods.

"Our village wasn't directly involved with the invasion. But to make sure we wouldn't fight back, the Germans took the men away in buses—to camps surrounded by high, chain-linked fences and barbed wire. It was bad for the women. They had no one. No one to protect them from the soldiers."

"Was it bad for you?'

"I survived. I worked in the Resistance. I could talk to the guards. I could speak German. So I would tell them stories and sneak in Greek words and things, things those standing nearby could pick up."

Silence.

The Greek doesn't want to talk about this. Shifts to the Lost City of Atlantis. Legends. Myths containing truth and wisdom. The Woman listens: leaning against him, under his arm. Head on his chest.

The phone rings. The Woman goes through the dining room. To the kitchen. His electric brown eyes follow her. Study her lanky legs in her parrot-green chinos. Climb her willowy arms sticking out from white short shirtsleeves. Lick her bronzed skin. Lose themselves in her thick, long, sun-streaked tawny hair. Linger on her fleecy, bold, yellow-gold vest.

"Hi ... fine. Raining here too. Was there a line up? ... Are the kids in bed? Mmhm ... Mmhm ... How're your mom and dad holding out? ... Did you manage to take the kids by yourself ... catch anything? ... They would like that ... How did they like sleeping in a tent? ... You—scared? ... after the garbage ... Really ... Mmhm ... Yeah ... yeah ... Well. I gotta go ... No! ... Yeah sure ... I gotta do my laundry, get ready for tomorrow. ... Okay. See ya Friday. I do too. Ba-bye."

Returning to the sofa. "They're coming home on Friday."

Silence.

They sit face to face. Silently, talk with their eyes. Kiss. Live coal. His mouth on hers.

Silence.

She says: "Tell me another story."

"I'm tired. It's hard work. Talking English. Tell me. Why did you want to take part in the Visitors Programme?"

"I wanted to meet Greeks. I'm a theologian."

His eyes question her.

She says: "At my church, our minister says Christians who live their faith are theologians. The Spirit guides them. Most people think the Holy Spirit is some kind of creative energy force, a divine goodness that exists inside us."

"You don't?"

"I think the Holy Spirit was the Woman at the Well. When Jesus breathed on the disciples, saying, 'Receive the Holy Spirit,' He was asking them to receive Her. She's the Paraclete, the Spirit of Truth, sent by the Father to testify on behalf of Jesus. People who say they are filled with the Holy Spirit aren't really. Not until they've accepted Her. As each of us unites with Her, the Holy Spirit gets greater."

"There's only one Holy Spirit."

"And that's me?"

He puts his mouth on hers. Pushes his tongue against hers. Probing. Rubbing the interior.

The phone rings. Breaks them apart.

"Oh hi … Fine. How are you? … Yes. Loved it. Thanks for suggesting it. I didn't see you there. Where were ya? … On the right. … Yes, I found the headphones. … Sure. I'll read on Sunday. What Scripture? … just the Gospel … you'll read the Psalm. Okay. Oh, by the way, are you driving in tomorrow? … Will Ed have room? … I did. My mom needs it tomorrow … no, she's picking it up. I'm leaving it in the driveway. Sure … five o'clock, outside the chapel at VST. Where's that? … behind the tent. Yesss, I'll be on time. Thanks, ba-bye."

Returning. "My minister."

"Are you going in … for the worship?"

Playing with her earring. Working the back up and down on the post. "No … I want to sleep in … I'm going in about ten—taking the bus. I was arranging for a ride home. How about you?"

Sitting down. "Are you planning to attend?"

The Greek shakes his head. Lights another cigarette. Inhaling. "I'm thirsty." Exhaling. "Will you get me a drink?"

"Sure. Coffee, beer?"

"Water … please."

In the kitchen.

It's dark. The Woman leans across the sink. Turns the light on. He watches her. From the sofa. Smoke rises about him. She turns the tap on. Lets the water run—the sound fills the silence.

She stands for a moment. Gazes at the rushing water. Right hand under left elbow. Thumb under chin. Digits curled. First index digit rubbing her lips.

She turns. Looks through the dining room into the living room. Inhales the smell. Tobacco. Greek cologne. Drinks his presence. Raven-black hair, combed straight back, receding slightly. Olive complexion. Forehead lines. Thick eyebrows. Bent earlobe. Broad nose. Deep lines centering nose. Wide bottom lip. Bare arms. Black downy hair on arms. Watch on left wrist. Wedding band.

She walks into the dining room. Past the sofa. Past his scent. To the china cabinet.

Chooses a crystal glass. Fills the glass. Returns to the sofa.

Hands him the glass.

His gold wedding ring clinks.

Fills her ears.

He puts the glass to his wide bottom lip. Welcoming the water. The moment. A gift.

"It's raining. It's not safe for you to drive back at night all by yourself."

"Sure it is."

"What if you have a breakdown?"

Outside the window. From the street comes the sound of the rain and the swish of a car.

"I've got a crazy idea. Why don't I stay over?"

She studies his face. His eyes. She looks deep down inside him. Her eyes thirst for a reason to say yes.

"Not in your husband's bed. I'll sleep in one of the children's."

Upstairs in the daughter's room.

The Woman and the Greek stand in the lighted doorway. Look into the darkened room. He suggests the Woman sleep in the single bed. That he sleep on the floor at her feet. A mischievous grin creeps onto his face.

The Woman turns away from the daughter's room.

From the shadows of the Woman's mind, an ancient Hebrew woman's image is projected. Ruth gleaning. Plotting with Naomi. Sleeping at the feet of Boaz. Choosing a new husband.

Invites the Greek across the hall—into the darkened master bedroom. He follows. She opens the closet. Gives him her husband's robe. Takes her robe. Enters en suite—turns light on—leaves—him—door ajar.

She returns. Dims light. Goes to the window. Opens it.

He's still there, outside the closet, silhouetted by moonlight. Waiting. Watching. Standing erect. Shoulders back. Stomach in. Chest out. Arms crossed. Right hand clutching left arm below elbow. Left hand over sex. Looking like a wise man in the Christmas pageant in her husband's brown velour bathrobe. Robust, with white and ruddy stripes on neck and sleeves.

Silence.

The Greek says in a low voice: "Ah … you are beautiful …"

Blue eyes engage with brown—the mystery there. Has she always loved him?

He places his left hand under her head. Draws her toward him, right hand embracing her. He feels it. Is afraid to want her. Afraid to need her. He says nothing. Her breath sweetly caresses him.

She is the one who turns. Takes him to her bed. Her face is fresh, young. Innocent. Her eyes search his, see his love and desire.

She unties her husband's bathrobe, opens it. Slips it to the floor..

Sees his sex. Ready. Lets her pink robe fall to the floor beside his.

His breath comes slowly. Over his bottom lip. She makes him lie down on the comforter.

The Woman sits beside his still body. On the bed. Cross-legged. Looks at his naked body. His uncircumcised sex. The puckered skin pitting and creasing the tiny hole in his side. Touches him there.

She asks in a hushed voice: "How did this happen?"

"I don't know. It happened … when I learned to kill Germans."

She kisses his side. He pulls her down on him. Kisses her as before, using his tongue. She pulls back. He nuzzles her neck, gives her a moment.

She presses her body against his.

He kisses her on the mouth again. Pushes his tongue harder against hers. Grabs her leg below the buttocks. His soft, powerful hand, gripping, slowly kneading, biting.

Her breath quickens. Her sex moistens. She bites his tongue. Rubs her burning bush against him. He moves from the bottom to the top. Cradles her in his arms. Careful not to crush her body. Mounts her. Pushes his sex between her thighs. Probes. Feeling for her rosy petals. Her wet channel. His wet dewy sex. Rubbing. Coaxing her rose to open. To blossom his sex.

She probes his mouth with her tongue. Bites his lips. Pushes her sex against his, feeling the heat; her breasts, sex, aching for his touch.

He comes, rolls over. She doesn't. Her mind is on fire. Racing.

Outside the window, from a distant street, comes the piercing sound of a siren.

The Woman feels it.

Deep down in her soul it calls her. The summer breeze is tender, reassuring in the sultry darkness.

The voice of love calls to her, *Song of Songs*, like it never has before:

> Open to me, my sister, my love,
> my dove, my perfect one;
> for my head is wet with dew …
> I had put off my garment;
> how could I put it on again? …
> My beloved thrust his hand into the opening,
> and my inmost being yearned for him.
> I arose to open to my beloved,
> and my hands dripped with myrrh

Set me as a seal upon your heart ...
for love is strong as death,
passion fierce as the grave.
Its flashes are flashes of fire ... [10]

The time is eight thirty. The Greek sits on the soft green and gold sofa. Lights a cigarette—pulling deeply on the first puff of the day—tilting his head back. Exhales slowly. Pushes out the smoke with his bottom lip. Like he does. Pushes up his suit sleeves.

He wants an atlas. She goes to find one. His eyes follow her, creep up long limbs sticking out beneath a slim straight skirt.

Returns with a large atlas tucked under her arm. Offers it to him. He cradles it on his knee. Caresses the embossed gold world on its blood-red cover. She leaves him there with the atlas in his powerful, soft hands. Hands unused to physical labour.

Familiar sounds and smells teem into the empty room. Of her. Running water. Crockery and cutlery. Cupboard doors bumping shut. Refrigerator door. Opening. Closing. Coffee perking. Toast popping. Toast buttered.

They breakfast in the living room. He breaks the toast apart with his hands. Dips his knife into the honey jar. Spreads the toasted bread. They eat and sip coffee side by side on the sofa.

Looking down. Playing with her earring.

"Surely this. Isn't adultery?"

His face. Stoic. Stares at her lukewarmly.

Silence.

An image comes into view. A woman from the Bible standing before a stoic rabbi. His angry followers saying: "In the law, Moses commanded us to stone such women. Now, what do you say?"[11]

Silence.

Three

Linda Vogt Turner

Seventeen years later.
July 2000

The Woman's home. The soft green and gold sofa. Near the window.

The Woman sits with a best-seller on her lap. The one she found at the church bookstore two years ago. Bold, parrot-green letters. A red circle. On a gold mat atop a red leafy cover. Stares up at her.

IT WAS ON
FIRE WHEN I
LAY DOWN
ON IT

○

ROBERT
FULGHUM

Right hand under left elbow. Thumb under chin. Digits curled. First index digit rubbing her lips.

Face radiant. Blue eyes bright. Turns to page three. Imagines that the newspaper story told there is the bait—a juicy tidbit of gossip. About a man rescued from a fire in an upstairs bedroom. Who.

When the fire responders ask: "How did it happen?" the Woman sees the Greek shrug, saying: "I don't know. It was on fire when I lay down on it."[12]

And then a friend adding his two bits: "Why do you laugh? Change the name, and the story is told of you."[13]

The Woman smiles. Nods ...
Laughs ...

The parrot-green chinos. On the gold sofa. That night. The fire within on her mattress. When the Greek lay down—the piercing sound of the siren rushing past her upstairs window. Seventeen years ago.

July 1983
The Lutheran Centre

The space set aside for the Women's Programme. Dubbed the Well. Out at the 6th Assembly of the World Council of Churches.

Women gathering.

La Source. Daily Visitors Programme ID tag pinned above her heart. The Woman takes a chair in front of the window. In front of the cardboard, pearl-studded, pencil-crayoned icon of the Holy City she hung in the window. With a clear view of Mercy Oduyoye. Mercy's beautiful face and head scarf.

Mercy speaks: "I am not even supposed to be interested in feminism.… The men say, 'African women are not oppressed,' and the men speak for us in these international forums. But we have a saying that the person who sleeps by the fire knows how hot the fire is …"[14]

Seventeen years later. Sitting on the soft green and gold sofa. The Woman remembers the Greek breaking the toasted bread. Dipping his knife into the honey jar. Asking for an atlas. The word adultery alarming the air. His lukewarm stare. The silence. A pall. Smoke filling the room.

That morning: July 27, 1983.

The Woman stands.

Tells the Greek she has to tidy the house. Put her lipstick on. That he has time for one more cigarette. That there is a bathroom downstairs opposite her office. Points the way. Takes the breakfast things out to the kitchen.

"We can't take the car. My mom needs it. She's coming for it today." She fidgets with her earring. "We need bus fare."

He reaches into his jacket for his wallet. "How much?"

"We need exact change. I'm not sure how much. I don't usually take the bus. I think it's two fifty.... If we give the driver a five-dollar bill that should do it. And if it's three, I've a dollar in change."

The Woman. Lipstick on. The smell of tobacco and Greek cologne in her hair. Goes out the way they came in. Through the garage. Past her tiny office.

Suit rumpled, the Greek walks out the front door. Raincoat under arm. Waits while the Woman backs her mom's '78 Ford out into the driveway.

The Woman wears an aquamarine jacket, jean skirt, leather sandals. Hair in a ponytail. Joins him on the porch, at the front door. Locks it. Drops key into straw bag with her books and papers.

They step onto the sidewalk. Him by the curb, her on his right. They do not touch.

It's a beautiful, cloudless summer morning. Children play in a distant yard. The joy, the laughter and the banter of boys and girls tumble into the street.

Up the street, as the bus pulls away from the curb: The Woman says. "Darn. We'll have to wait another half-hour."

He says. "Good. That'll give us more time."

They talk. He's fifty. Arranged marriage. Married twenty years.

The Woman is thirty-two. Married young. Writes essays, poems and revelations. "Can I write to you? Send you my work? Will you show my work to Dimitri? Defend my ideas?"

The Greek, raincoat in left arm, places his left arm behind his back. Steps forward onto his right leg, placing it in front of the left. Bows forward, sweeping his right arm from his heart over the ground—rising to her. "My dear, it will be my honour and privilege."

"Will you write back?"

"No, your husband won't like it."

"My husband won't mind."

The Greek tightens his face. Becomes stoic.

She argues—trying not to show signs of anger and hurt. Her desire for the Greek is strong. Tries to convince him that her husband will not be jealous, that theirs is an open marriage.

Further up the street. Other Christians on the bus route. ID tags around their necks. Bleached cotton bags over their shoulders. Get on the bus.

At the bus stop, the Greek and the Woman look up the street. For the bus. A man in shirtsleeves carries a briefcase, walks toward the bus stop. Sees the Greek dressed in a business suit. His brow furrows—spotting the raincoat. Looks up at the sky.

In a window of a nearby basement home—with a view of the bus stop—a homemaker washes her breakfast dishes. Her TV is on. Tuned to the station reporting on the World Council of Churches. It projects a picture from yesterday of a Greek man standing at a plenary microphone. She observes the couple outside, waiting for the bus.

"What's he doing here? Our church wasn't asked to billet."

The Greek sees the man in shirtsleeves walking toward them. And tenses.

The Woman turns to see why. As the man comes closer, the Woman says: "Hi, Terry. I thought you and Louise moved."

"We did. I'm renting up the street."

Silence.

The Woman plays with her stud earring. Works the back up and down on the post. Toward and away from her ear. "This is my uncle. He's from Europe. We're going to take in the sights."

Terry nods. Looks away. Up the street.

Silence.

Cars on the street whiz by. Stir the air. Flutter the Woman's hair.

The Greek looks across the street. Notices a sign: it beckons all to Sunday worship. Her eyes follow his.

She sees it, hears its hum on the pavement. Tires are weighted down with its heavy load.

She steps forward to the curb. The men move behind her. The bus brings a rush of wind, pushes the bangs off her face.

The three climb on. She queries the bus driver. How does she get out to the university? Where should she transfer? What buses should she take? How much is the fare?

The Greek reaches into his breast pocket for his wallet. Gives the driver a five-dollar bill. The Woman takes a left window seat in the center of the bus. The Greek takes the adjoining aisle seat. His shoulder touches hers. He whispers into her ear. She whispers back.

When the neighbour drops his coins into the box, he watches the Woman and her uncle. Walks past them. Sits in an aisle seat a few rows away. Beside a woman with a bleached cotton bag printed with the Greek word oikoumene.

A few days later. The children are at the lake with their grandparents. Her husband is home now. Working the graveyard shift. The Woman has their car. The Rally Sport.

It's now August 1983.

The second week of the Assembly. She takes the Rally Sport. Out to the university. Wants to see the Greek. She is dressed in aquamarine slacks that match her jacket, the one she wore that morning they climbed the bus together. Egyptian-blue cotton shirt with wine-coloured stripes. Auburn sun-streaked hair long and straight. She spends the morning at the space for women at the Lutheran Centre–The Well. Her pencil crayon cardboard model of the Holy City is there in the window, an iconic geometric sphere. The twelve gates. Studded with twelve pearls. Coloured pencil crayoned triangles represent stained glass—the twelve jewels edged in gold. Dazzling. Jasper red. Topaz yellow. Sapphire blue. Carnelian orange. Emerald green. Jacinth purple. Amethyst violet.

At the Lutheran Centre–The Well, programme participants gather, lift up women's work and concerns. As the female speaker talks about South Africa, the Woman thinks about that morning, last week when she showed the Greek the icon, the one she donated when she registered for the programme. When they got off the bus here, when she ushered him in. Stood off to the side. Read the posted daily events. He studied her craft. Before they parted, she to the Visitors Programme here, he to the Plenary programme. Kissed her eyes with his. From across the room. An invisible wall sprang up between them. She not Greek, a philosopher or a great teacher and council advisor. Merely a servant girl with no university degree. A volunteer. A mom who served hot dogs at school. Fundraised for cancer and the Red Cross. Read the lesson at church. When they let her. Taught Sunday school.

His electric brown eyes—continue—to kiss her soul.

Deep down she knows. *We are the Source of all life. We shed blood that issues from our wombs. Without our blood and water, there would be no new generation. We should have a say. Our leadership should be recognized.*

The Woman thinks about another time.
In Delta.
In May 1979.

Women are gathered for Bible study in the old worship space set aside.

For Sunday school. With hospital curtains. For rooms.

The Woman's children are with the minister's wife in the old vestry. In the old white country-style church with the wooden creaky floors and coloured glass windows.

The Reverend Mr. Caldwell is leading them. The study book has a red flame on the cover. The first lesson is on John's Gospel, chapter four. The Samaritan Woman at the Well. The book and the study group insist the Samaritan Woman was a slut who needed to repent.

Later that day, in the Woman's home, her children are napping. The Woman sits on the gold and green brocade sofa.

29

Opens her Bible.

"The Sa mar i tan woman said to him, 'How is it that you a Jew, ask a drink of me, a woman of Sa mar i a?'" (Jews do not share things in common with Sa mar i tans.)[15]

The Woman thinks: *It's curious the way the text separates the syllables. I can't believe the study group assumed she was a slut.*

> The conversation.
>
> Jesus answered her, "If you knew the gift of God, and who it is that is saying to you, 'Give me a drink,' you would have asked him, and he would have given you living water."
>
> The woman said to him, "Sir, you have no bucket, and the well is deep. Where do you get that living water? Are you greater than our ancestor Jacob, who gave us the well, and with his sons and his flocks drank from it?"
>
> "Everyone who drinks of this water will be thirsty again, but those who drink of the water that I will give will never be thirsty. The water that I will give them will become in them a spring of water gushing up to eternal life."[16]

From the sofa, the Woman looks up. Listens. For her napping children. Upstairs.

Silence.

> The woman said to him, "Sir, give me this water, so that I may never be thirsty or have to keep coming here to draw water."
>
> "Go, call your husband, and come back."
>
> "I have no husband."
>
> "You are right in saying, 'I have no husband'; for you have had five husbands, and the one you

have now is not your husband. What you have said
is true!"

"Sir, I see that you are a prophet. Our ancestors
worshipped on this mountain, but you say that the
place where people worship is in Jerusalem."[17]

With her elbow on the sofa. Thumb under chin. Digits curled.
First index digit rubbing her lips. The Woman muses. Like a poet.
Eyes drift across the room. At the Carpet. Rich. Brown. Carved.
Different shades. Like the earth. Hide things—fluff, crumbs, dirt.

*Jesus, a traveler knew the woman had five husbands and the man
she was living with was not really her husband.*

*I pointed out Jesus was most likely speaking figuratively ... that the
five husbands were the first five books of the Bible ... the Torah.*

*Reverend Caldwell and the others looked at me ... as if I were on
Mars.*

Rubs her lips again.

More likely ... she too was speaking figuratively. The man *we all
live with is not our husband. God is. I should have said that.*

*Or the Samaritan woman could have been widowed and the man
she was living with could have been her brother or her father?*

But then again, how did Jesus know that?

Stares out across the room.

*Reverend Caldwell said it was common knowledge that the nation
of Samaria was adulterous ... no respectful woman of the day would
go to the Well at noon ... alone.*

The Woman rubs her hand on the sofa cushion. Feels the
brocade, the nubby green inside the silky gold.

"Woman, believe me, the hour is coming when you
will worship the Father neither on this mountain
nor in Jerusalem. You worship what you do not
know; we worship what we know, for salvation is
from the Jews. But the hour is coming and is now

31

here, when the true worshippers will worship the
Father in spirit and truth, for the Father seeks such
as these to worship him. God is spirit, and those
who worship him must worship in spirit and truth.

"I know that Messiah is coming" (who is called
Christ). "When he comes, he will proclaim all
things to us."

"I am he, the one who is speaking to you."[18]

Four years later.
August 1983.

The Lutheran Centre Well.

The talk.

The morning sun kisses the room. The Woman doesn't know
what to think. About life. South Africa. Nelson Mandela. Desmond
Tutu.

Knows Desmond Tutu is a bishop. He's here. She's heard him
speak. About Apartheid. Listens more intently. Thirsty to know
what men and educated people know. About life. Politics. Race.
Gender. Apartheid.

At noon the Woman picks up her straw bag. Goes to the Sub.
There are people everywhere; the joy, the laughter, the sounds of
cutlery and crockery spill outside from inside—like that other day.
When she'd turned. At the sound of the Jewish music for peace.
Had met the Greek.

Like before, lines of friendly people wait to enter. Colour and
gender barriers seem forgotten.

The Woman stands off to the side. Waits for the Greek. On the
path leading to the Sub. In yellow shirt he appears. Like Apollo,
Greek god of the sun. She young. Leggy. Tanned and beautiful.
Like Sol, the Norse goddess of the Sun. Conquered. Not defeated.
Shoots forward. A tiny sunbeam subduing a goliath. The Greek sees

her. Turns. Heads toward her. Kisses her. On both cheeks. Breathes. The scent of the Woman. Baby powder and musk. Chanel No. 5.

He's meeting someone. No time for lunch. Suggests dinner at six. Like before.

The Woman returns to the lines of friendly people. Picks up a tray. Behind her, a grey-bearded man dressed in black priestly robes picks up a tray.

Has he seen her speaking with the Greek? Just now.

He's Orthodox. Says: "My dear. Would you do me the honour of dining with me?"

She recognizes him. He spoke on the place of women in the church. In the afternoon plenary. Feminists opposed his views. She says yes.

Selects a table by the wall. Sits looking out across the room. To the window. He joins her. Sits by her side.

The Woman is naïve. She knows little about politics or life. Her naivety protects her. Later it will embarrass her. Work against her.

That first day, when she met the Greek, she dined with members of the PLO. Terrorists.

Wall of separation. Between brown and white. Male and female. Beyond her everyday experience. She is a woman of privilege. Her own person. Like a goddess. Virginal. No man intimidates, possesses, rules over her. The Woman knows nothing of terrorist action, domination, cruelty.

Her luncheon companion introduces himself. He's a metropolitan. An Orthodox bishop and teacher from Athens. They talk about priestly things. He tells her that Orthodox priests marry but bishops don't.

"Bishops have many duties and responsibilities. They have no time for family life. It's unfair to the family to go without the support they need."

She agrees. Likes this man. Looks into his grey-bearded face. Kind brown eyes. Asks about divorce.

"The Orthodox Church believes marriage is indissoluble. Everlasting. But the Church also recognizes that couples are human and capable of making mistakes. So the Church will tolerate up to a third marriage."

The Woman thinks this is fair. She is about to say something when an older woman dressed in polyester slacks, white socks and sneakers approaches the table, says, "Do you mind if I join you?"

The Bishop replies, "Yes. We're having a private conversation."

Astonished. She leaves with a resigned sigh.

The Woman and the Bishop finish eating. Move outside. Toward flag pole square where the red and white Canadian flag sails in the wind. Tall and proud over the expanse of lush green grass, blue sea and mountains, into the sky. Augments the Woman's sense of freedom. She speaks freely to issues separating East and West. Male and female: marriage. Divorce. Working moms. Abortion. Ordination. Sacraments. The book of Revelation.

The grey-bearded Bishop listens. Says: "Sacraments are secrets. We have a responsibility to keep the sacraments. To be good stewards. We mustn't reveal them."

"Why? People need to know these secrets. How can we be good stewards and not reveal these secrets?"

"People need mystery. If there is no mystery and all is revealed, people will take their salvation for granted."

The Woman disagrees. "People need a clear example of how to live. Christ came to be that example. To help us believe in ourselves and to see that we need to talk and discuss things. Secrets lead to mistrust, suspicion, fear, hatred. Questions lead to dialogue, conversation, acceptance, collaboration, consensus."

The Bishop walks briskly. The Woman enjoys the pace. His priestly authority draws out her spiritual knowledge.

"People need to know all there is to know. The truth sets people free. The seven spirits that stand in front of the throne in the opening chapter of the book of Revelation are not sacraments or secrets. Rather they are words that reveal the truth."

With his soft dove eyes, the Bishop questions her. His black priestly robe, the flag sailing in the wind give her a freedom she has never known before.

She says: "To find the truth, one ought to start by asking if. You see one needs to start by supposing something. Like Descartes. If you and I are both walking along. Then we are. Then we need to ask other questions, such as, 'Who is the person sitting next to me? What is happening around us? Where are we? Why are we here? When are we going to stop walking? How are we going to know when and where we're going to stop?'"

The Bishop's face is gentle. His smiling lips, a soft pink ribbon of satisfaction. Between moustache and beard.

She quotes Luke 8:17: "Nothing is secret that shall not be made manifest."[19]

They come to a bench. He motions with his hand for her to sit. Sits beside her. She continues her talk about the book of Revelation. How people have lost the secret to its understanding. And how some people think Armageddon and the apocalypse will actually and literally take place.

The Woman remembers Dimitri's reaction that night she met the Greek. His conviction.

"Moses said he heard God speaking to him from a burning bush, and I believe him."

The Woman wants the Bishop to see the Holy Ground that roots and sustains the burning bush. Takes out a large manila envelope from her straw bag. Draws a square on it. Puts a large circle in the square. Draws a line from the top left corner to the bottom right. She wants to show the Bishop what she has figured out, reading the Bible for herself and thinking about nothing ... a nought, a web of interwoven characters who know that nothing is the very secret ... that shall reveal and make all things known, for those who know that the first number of all numbers is zero.

She begins by explaining how she assumed the Holy City was the global city—the world. From that assumption she looked at scripture and tested her assumption with the scripture that says the Holy City lies foursquare with a measure of 12,000 stadia and has a partition of 144 cubits according to the measure of an angel.[20]

He nods for her to continue.

"If the diameter of the circle, the nought, within the square is 8,400, the diagonal of the square will be 12,000. If you divide 144 by 45.72 centimetres, the metric measure of a small cubit, you will get 3.14. Pi ... 8400 x 3.14 = 26,376. Multiply that number by a Roman man's pace measuring 1.5 metres ... the circumference will be 39,564. Rounded up to the nearest 1,000, the circle will measure 40,000 kilometres.

The Bishop doesn't ask her: "Why centimetres and metres?"

She would have said: "Because Abraham and Sarah's son, Isaac, sewed a crop in faith and received a hundredfold harvest.[21] As their descendants, we have inherited this blessing. If we sow the seeds of faith, we will receive a hundredfold harvest as a tenfold blessing to bless others with. Together, we will see the new heaven and the new earth that God has in store for us. Then with our faith renewed and confirmed, we will realize God's promise of eternal life and know ... that heaven and earth are one."

The Bishop simply smiles.

She flips the envelope over.

Draws.

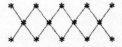

Continues. "The Jewelled City comes out of heaven. It lies foursquare. Look and see how. It has twelve gates, each adorned with a jewel. Represented here by a star. When I draw a line from each star, I get diamond shapes. Squares on end. The three inner squares are easy to see. The two outer open upended squares unite at the top and bottom gate or star to form the fourth square."

The Bishop, eyes, face smiling, reaches beneath his gown into his pocket. For a pen. A notepad. Writes his name, address, telephone number on a red, lined sheet. Hands it to the Woman. "When you come to Greece, you'll need my name."

Casually, the Woman tosses the sheet into her straw bag.

He nudges her shoulder with his fist. "I'm serious. Keep this somewhere safe, because when you come to Greece you must look me up."

They part.

Alone. The Woman reflects on the net she herself has drawn. The Bishop's response.

I'm a housewife … how can I ever go to Greece? My husband is not really a believer. It's a fight to get him to church. I've never even been to college. We budget our money. There's not enough for separate holidays. And even if I could set aside some, how could I explain why I wanted to go to Greece?

Later that evening.

The Woman and the Greek are in her and her husband's '79 Rally Sport. The one the Greek called a dangerous sportster model that other evening. She's worried about the gas. If she uses too much her husband will wonder why. She decides to drive out to Burnaby. To Central Park. Away from tourists. World Council visitors.

She parks the car in the parking lot in front of the trees facing Boundary Road. They get out of the car and walk back toward the trees. He wants to touch her. Kiss her. His desire is strong. He embraces her there in the park. Kisses her hard on the mouth. In front of the other people out walking.

She's suddenly very conscious of the differences that separate their two worlds. He's a man of fifty dressed in a sport coat, wearing sunglasses. She's only thirty-two. Tells him, "People in Canada don't kiss in public. It's just not done."

He leads her off the path. Into the trees. The wilderness.

Four

Linda Vogt Turner

Canberra. Thursday, February 7
The year is 1991.
The time is eight thirty.

A colossal tent sits there on the lawn, bold and white, in the middle of a wide expanse. Everything is wide open. Like a wedding banquet. There is a droning hum. A rhythmic clack-clack-clack of the didgeridoo. Mixed with chants of the Kyrie. Rich voices singing "Santo, Santo, Santo." Beckoning people in suits, dresses and summer leisure. Like that other time in Vancouver.

There are fresh fragrances of dew and grass mingling with the scent of burning leaves. They're preparing for worship. The season is Lent. Local television crews are setting up. Naked chalked bodies in red skirts and headbands focus attention. An immense yellow parachute with red cloth streamers billows up and pushes out a pink narrow banner. On it. A silver cup of red. A flaming silver cross. On it hangs a heart of gold, a light and five parchments. Facing out. On the left. A rainbow snake banner. A white man strums, a black man bongos. On the right an aboriginal priest stands. In white clerical dress. Another with mitre and stole. Women and plants behind them. Some wearing black dresses and red headbands. Others in colourful dress. One black-clad woman, head-banded in red, threads a red ribbon through her fingers. Stands amid the chalked bodies. A long table draped in white in front. At one end. Red-flamed cactus arms. Rows of chairs on the grass wait to be filled. Thousands talking or listening. Like before, in Vancouver. Hymns, prayers each in a different language—calling. Come, Holy Spirit—Renew the Whole Creation.

February 16

Day ten. The colossal white wedding tent beckons.

Like Vancouver, the icon of the Trinity comes into view and takes form. Where the aboriginal bishop stood, days ago. Comes the Orthodox grey beard, black robe, stove hat, gold cross.

40

It is a marriage. The Father issues the invitation. The table is set, the wine poured for the Orthodox. Thousands told they can only watch. Fill the chairs, stand at the doors. Priests. Holy fathers stand in front of the rows.

The Greek enters. Older now. White hair. Respected theologian, peacemaker, teacher, council member. Cameras follow him. He strides past the Woman, sitting in the middle of a row. On the grass. Seven rows from the front. People. Chairs. Rows. Encircle her.

She looks up. To her right. Sees the Greek in the aisle as he passes.

He sees her. Stoic. Resolute. He takes a seat. Ahead of her. In the empty reserved row. In front of the Priest.

The sound of her heart beats in her ears. Every nerve and muscle pushes her to the right. Past those like her. Told to watch. She looks like a girl. Tiny waist. Tawny hair. Desert-brown dress. Skinny, sun-tanned legs and arms. Sticking out. Her Wedgwood blue and white diamond shawl. Draped over one shoulder. Covering her heart. Her ID tag. With the word Mrs. in front of her name.

The Woman makes her way forward. Her heart beats in her ears. Past those told to watch. Past the Greek's silence, his stoic presence. Calls her. To the VIP row. The Priest. The Eucharist. She approaches the Greek. Earth-brown eyes meet sky-blue ones. Places her left arm behind her back. Steps forward onto her right leg, placing it in front of the left one. Bows forward, sweeping her right arm from her heart over the ground—rising to him. As he did at the bus stop that morning. In Vancouver.

The Greek. Stoic. Says nothing.

She turns. Face to face with the Priest, who asks. "What is your name?"

Tells him only her first name. He offers the tiny spoon. With the bits of bread and wine. She drinks from its tiny well.

Did anyone notice? See what I just did?

Turns.

A TV camera. Stares in her face. Moves out of the way. Lets her pass. She goes back. Pushes past twenty or so others. Told to watch. To her seat. Sky-blue eyes watchful. The tent explodes with a cacophony of voices. The Greek and others leave their chairs. On a walkabout.

The Woman's heart races. *What's going on? Have I caused this?* Sees the Greek calmly taking pictures.

Surely this is a Greek thing. People in Canada don't leave their seats, take pictures during the Eucharist.

Asks the people sitting beside her what's going on. They shrug. She sees the Greek stop in front of the Rainbow Snake banner. On a pole. At the front. To her right. He lingers. Studies it.

Why?

The Woman does not know. Her name means snake in old German. Why the Rainbow Serpent is revered in Aboriginal theology. That the dream spirit is the serpent who emerges from her underground sleep to free other snake like spirits. That Muchalinda is the legendary snake-like being of Thailand who protects Buddha with her shawl-like hood. That the shawl she bought at the World Vision booth was made in Thailand.

Those who know. See her snake past the others in her row. Join the Greek. Standing. In front of the colourful aboriginal designed snake banner on a pole.

The Woman knows Moses made a bronze, fiery serpent and set it on a standard.[22]

A flag standard … a banner pole …

The Woman imprints it in the deep recesses of her mind. Her skull. Later she'll remember and know.

That Moses made the fiery serpent into a brazen figure and lifted her up so that all would notice and be saved.

Beside the Greek—studying the snake—she wonders, *What have I done?*

Fidgeting with her earring, she says: "Are you free? Can we go for coffee and talk?"

"No. The service is not over."

"Will you come sit with me?"

"Not now. Later. I'll meet you. Where will you be?"

"In the Bible study."

"I'll come for you. We'll go for coffee."

A voice booms forth from the mike. "Everyone please exit the tent. Go outside to your home groups."

Outside. The Woman finds the other Canadians. The delegates chat. She's alone: an accredited visitor. Other visitors she's met, Simeonca, Josephine, Hector are with their groups.

The sun embraces the Woman. Comforts her. Calms her. She tries to join in with the others.

Why are they ignoring me? Is it because of the Mrs. on my name tag? Does it label me as traditional ... a homemaker ... non-feminist? Surely not. I'm glad I met Simeonca and Josephine from Cameroon ... on that pre-assembly tour. They have degrees.

The Woman stands off by herself. Looks around for a familiar face. Bewildered and lost.

It was good of Simeonca to say, "Nous sommes ensemble ..." to the guy at the registration desk. I had to translate. She told him that she and Josephine couldn't understand his Australian ... "Mais ... nous pouvons la comprendre ..."

Grabs the folded edge of her shawl.

Me ... with my limited French and my clear British-Canadian accent. Included in the seats reserved for the VIP wives in the plenary. Does this make me ... anti-feminist?

Marion, a delegate from BC walks by. The Woman smiles. Marion does not stop. Looks right past her.

Good. I met Hector last Sunday when the Greek went off with that younger woman. Hector's a Baptist delegate from the states ... sits at the same table as the Greek.

Finally the Woman sees Hal. He's a minister from Eastern Canada. He waves to the Woman. Comes over. Stands beside her. Says: "Do you know what's going on?

"No."

He takes off his hat, scratches his head. Says: "An international woman dressed just like you was served the Eucharist. The tent. It's in an uproar. People are on fire."

Blushing, the Woman quickly defends herself: "Galatians 3:28 says, 'There is neither Jew, nor Greek, slave nor free, male nor female, for [we] are all one in Christ Jesus.' [23]So I went forward and the priest served me."

"Several of us, thinking the same, went forward too. We were turned back."

Hal looks at the Woman. Her scarf. Where her ID tag should be.

She says nothing. Not sure how much Hal knows. Why the Priest served her. Did the Priest just assume she was Orthodox? Did he see her bow like a man to the Greek as if he was the second person in the Trinity? Did anyone see her do that? Did Hal?

The Woman looks at Hal. A middle-aged Canadian man. Runners. Dockers. Golf shirt. Hat.

Minister with the Canadian delegation.

Hal would know his scripture. Would know Philippians 2:10 … that "at the name of Jesus every knee should bend in heaven and earth and under the earth …"[24]

The Woman doesn't ask him.

Knows the problem with that scripture. Standing on that scripture. Banners waving. Europeans colonized pagans. Indigenous cultures. Women. Silenced them. Ignored their tears. Prayers. Visions. Dreams.

Wants Hal to tell her he's proud of her. For standing up for what she believes.

Wants a hug. Some kind of reassurance.

The name of Jesus trumps all. His. Hers. Finding it buried in the Story. Trusting it, unlocks the Gospel. Anoints Christians to preach good news to the poor. Proclaim release to the captives, and recovery of sight to the blind, to let the oppressed go free.[25]

A voice from the mike booms forth. "Because the Orthodox have been too busy celebrating the marriage of heaven and earth, we're out of time. The noon debate with Professor Chung Hyun Kyung has been cancelled. Please go directly to your programmes."

A cacophony of noise erupts. Male and female feminist delegates are angry.

Professor Kyung is female, a Korean Presbyterian theologian, educated in the West. A keynote speaker. She led the opening plenary theme the second day, in the Convention Centre's Royal Theatre. Twenty-five hundred official delegates, advisors and accredited visitors sat captive. Watched. A pretty, dainty Korean. Evoke a feminine Holy Spirit. Light on fire. Names of exploited women on small bits of paper. Juggle them. Ash fall. Almost naked, chalked male bodies dance. Behind. Beside. Christians rise. In ovation. Many shouting angry accusations of idolatry, syncretism and doctrinal error reach the Greek. Push him forward to debate the question of the gender of the Holy Spirit.

Now with the scheduled debate called off, the question hangs in the air.

The tent empties. Waits for visitors to come for the Bible study. The Woman takes a seat. At the back. Near an exit. Fishes a folded piece of paper from her blue jean bag with the saffron handles. It's the paper the Greek gave her. Several days ago. After the opening worship the first day, February 7. When the Woman looked for him.

45

Five

February 7.

In the colossal tent.

She looks for him. His raven-black hair. Searches the faces. Olive complexion. Forehead lines. Thick eyebrows. Bent earlobe. Broad nose. Deep lines centering nose. Wide bottom lip. After the hymns, prayers each in a different language, the Woman takes the path to the food queues. Stands to one side. Waits. Watches. A man with white hair walk past her. The way he walks speaks to her.

Without thinking, her willowy legs bolt after him. She taps him on the shoulder.

He turns around. Their eyes meet. He hugs her. Long and hard. She smells him. Drinks in his scent. Says: " I've cut my hair."

"You're even more beautiful…. In what capacity are you here?"

"I'm an accredited visitor."

Looking at her ID tag. The Greek sees the title Mrs. before her name. "It's over."

The Woman stifles her devastation. *I've come all this way. For the "spring of water gushing up to eternal life."*[26]

"We need to talk. Can we meet?"

The Greek steps back. Still. Looking directly at her. "I'm a delegate, on the central committee. I have many time restraints. Your schedule is more flexible. Wait for me tomorrow morning outside the tent. Wait only fifteen minutes. Before worship. If I can get away I'll come."

The next morning: the Woman sees two green chairs outside the tent. Like children use in school. Metal legs. Hard plastic seats. Separate narrow backs. Under a grove of willow trees. She sits down. Sees the Greek approaching. Stands up. He kisses her on both cheeks as Greeks do—a greeting of peace. Motions for them to sit down.

She gets right to the point. Explains that she does not want a romantic relationship with him. That she wants a professional relationship.

He asks: "What do you mean? Professional?"

"I want a legitimate role. I want to be included as an equal. To lift up women's voices and their concerns in the wider church. To bring unity to the Church. Ecumenism."

People walk past them. On the way to worship. See them sitting alone. Face to face. In the middle of a wide expanse. Under the shade of the willows.

The Greek looks at his watch. "How can I help?"

"If we could work on a project together, we could get some cross-pollination happening?

"What do you mean 'pollination'?"

"People need new thoughts ... new ideas ... from outside their own garden ... their own culture ... to impregnate ... infuse each other's crops to bring about an abundant harvest of ideas."

He looks at her. Smiles. Remembers that day at noon. In Vancouver. Her fire. When she spoke about man and woman. Telling him he was a helper of mankind, a woman. Says: "Can you come here and wait for me every day? When I can, I'll come, we'll talk some more."

The Woman nods. They part.

The next day the Woman waits. Stands. Near the willows. Several worship leaders pass by. Notice her. She notices them.

Silence.

The Greek does not come.

The next day and the next. She waits. The Greek does not come.

Later, after worship, the Woman follows the path to the food queues. Booths are set up. She stops at the World Vision booth. Finds a Wedgwood blue and white diamond cotton shawl. Immediately she sees the pattern. The pattern she described to the Bishop in Vancouver. The one from the book of Revelation.

The Woman knows the passage by heart.

> And I saw the holy city, new Jerusalem, coming
> down out of heaven from God, prepared as a bride
> adorned for her husband ...

"Behold, the dwelling of God is with men...they shall be his people, and God himself will be with them; he will wipe away every tear from their eyes."

And he said ... "It is done! I am the Alpha and the Omega, the beginning and the end. To the thirsty I will give water without price from the fountain of the water of life."[27]

The Woman buys the cotton shawl. With the diamond pattern. Folds it. Inside out. Lengthwise. She likes the colour better. The blue stands out. Instead of the white. Drapes it over her left shoulder. Frees her right shoulder, for her dark blue jean and saffron oikumene bag.

She turns, sees the Greek. On the path. Coming toward the booth. Where the Woman is. His companion is female, young and beautiful. The Woman steps into the path. Greets them.

The Greek does not kiss the Woman on both cheeks. Does not introduce her to his female companion.

The Greek's companion feels the tension. The need. For the Greek's privacy. Walks on ahead. Stops. Waits.

The Woman says to the Greek: "It's Sunday. Are you free?"

"No. I have to spend the day with the Greeks."

The Woman's face falls. *I've deluded myself. I'm not the living Magdalene, the Holy Spirit. He's not the living Christ. He let me think that, just to score.*

The Woman blinks back her tears. "Is this something that you do ... when you travel ... pick up young women?"

"No. Believe me. You and me ... I've never done anything like that before. If people knew. I'd be in a lot of trouble.... Will you wait for me tomorrow?"

Silence.

"Yes."

"Good."

The Woman's left hand clasps her shawl. She watches him go. Off with the younger woman. To spend the day with the Greeks.

50

Silence.

A man from India comes up to the Woman. Bombards her with information. Can she help him? Sign his petition. Children are being exploited in India.

She just can't think. Tries to listen. Find a way to disengage.

A Hispanic man senses her distress. Comes forward. Leads her. Away. To brown tables and chairs set aside. The kind found in school gyms.

They sit.

Tears overtake the Woman. She looks for a tissue. Dabs the tears on her cheeks, under her eyes. Careful not to smudge her makeup. Blows her nose.

His name is Hector. He's from San Francisco. A Baptist. Lay delegate. Sits at the same table in the plenary as the Greek.

Hector's smile is friendly. His eyes soft and kind. His shirt white and embroidered. Hangs loose. Outside his jeans.

The Woman thinks of him as a brother. Someone of her own generation—a flower child—from San Francisco.

She confides in Hector. Tells him how she met the Greek. That she has been writing to him. Sending him her work. Her poems. Devotionals. The Woman shows Hector her shawl. Explains its significance in light of the Assembly's theme: Come, Holy Spirit—Renew the Whole Creation. Takes the blue jean bag. Off her knee. Places it on the table. Fishes out one of her poems.

The Mistress

Exploited, polluted
lacking divinity
the earth clings
to the feet of the Master
and begs for His mercy

she in innocent grace
gives freely all she has
bloody and exhausted
from the Master's battles
still she touches His robe

her perfume once like nard
and so graciously poured
at the feet of her King
has turned toxic and sour
she is cursed and ignored

she is unclean and told
to repent, she who loves
and forgives much, must change
no more must she allow
man or beast liberty.

A sad thing this is
she loves her wilderness
and those who delight her
walking all over her
wandering, living free

her life once beautiful
long like a woman's hair
is now cropped and quite short
sophisticated man knows
yet is not inspired.

How can she get out from
under the Master's feet?
How can she sin no more
or teach those who mistreat
and malign her fine work?

Who will notice this sage
and appreciate her?
She babbles and speaks plain
to the prophets and those
who heed the silent well.

Man's salvation is tied
to her and her mission
to be our dear Mistress
to set at liberty
all those who are oppressed.

If we liberate Her
She will teach us,
Her wind and water will kiss us
and we will faithfully
with heart and mind respond.

Hector gently places her poem in front of her on the table.
She feels his compassion.
"Have you any more?"
The Woman pulls out two more.
Hector watches her. Tawny curly bobbed hair. Willowy arms
reach into her bag.
He takes the poems. Places them on the table—reads slowly.
She plays with her earring. Pushes the stud back and forth on
the post. Feels his concentration.
"Can I show these to my committee group?"

Later that night.

It's very hot in her tiny hotel room. Clad in a grey, spaghetti-strap T-shirt nightie. The woman turns on the water in the shower. Lets the cold water run. Creates a breeze from the open window and door. Sits down. Under the window. On the bed. Finds the manila envelope that holds her work. She fishes out a Sunday school story she embellished for her Grade four class. To act out for their parents. For the Christmas Pageant at St. John's. She changed the ending. To help people see how the female Jesus in Samaria comes into the story to make room in people's hearts for the gift of God. The Woman is sure she mailed it to the Greek. She sent him everything before Canberra.

The Window of Charvel

Today's story is about a man named Antoine, a stained-glass window and a woman with a shawl. The story takes place in the olden days when churches used candles instead of electric lights, and stained-glass windows were the only Bibles people had.

One Christmas Eve, 30 pieces of silver went missing from the church of Charvel. Antoine, an apprentice stained-glass window maker, was falsely accused of taking them. No one believed Antoine when he insisted he did not take the silver. Antoine was exiled; he was sent to Paris.

The Woman looks around her tiny hotel room. A prisoner of heat. *Canberra like Paris. Place of exile. Brick homes. Concrete buildings. Wide avenues. Fountains. Works of art. No stained-glass churches. Flies.*

A cool waft of air caresses the Woman's shoulder. From the cooling concrete outside. She imagines Paris. *The Louvre. La Tour*

54

Eiffel. Street cafes with their caned chairs. Works of great art. Stained glass. Notre Dame. Sacré-Cœur. Moulin Rouge. Jazz.

She looks down at the typewritten page from the Sunday school curriculum she made subtle changes to.

> Some years later, when Antoine had become a famous stained-glass window maker, the people of Charvel went to Paris. They went to Antoine and told him they now knew he had not stolen the 30 pieces of silver. The villagers then asked Antoine to design a stained-glass window as a gift for the church of Charvel. And so Antoine did.

The Woman rises from the bed. Goes to the toilet. Turns the shower off. Returns to the bed.

> But when the last piece of glass was in place, the people were very confused and disappointed. The window designed by the most famous Antoine (the stained-glass window maker) was dull and drab. It didn't gleam in the sunlight or glow in the candlelight. The workers were sent to Paris to learn from Antoine why the window was dark and lifeless. The workers asked Antoine if some terrible mistake on their part had caused this. Antoine answered them: "Tell the people of Charvel that on Christmas Eve, when someone brings a worthy gift to the altar, the window will shine with a beautiful light, but not until then."

She brushes a fly away. Extends her right hand and arm from her chest up over her face. Like people in Canberra do. Creates a soft breeze. The Woman thinks about the Christmas pageant. The other teachers. How they dismissed her attempts to show how comforters, shawls, and aprons were icons. Faded and worn, reflecting the passion, the love and light of God.

On Christmas Eve everyone came to church with a gift, hoping their gift would prove worthy and so light up the window.

The Lord of the castle brought a bag of gold. The Lady of the castle brought a silver bowl filled with roses. And the children from the castle brought candy and toys for the orphans. But the window remained as dark as midnight.

Several times that night a woman wearing a thin, faded shawl had tried to come in to pray and to worship God. But the men guarding the door saw a woman unknown to them with no gift in her hand, wearing a faded shawl. They turned her away, thinking her to be a woman of ill renown: a gypsy woman, nobody of any worth.

In the stifling heat the Woman remembers another story from the Bible. The story of Ruth. A travelling widow. From Moab. A foreigner. A Gentile. A gleaner. Lying at the feet of Boaz. Great-grandmother of David and ancestor of Jesus. Wanting. Status. Redemption.

The respectable women of the village brought homemade bread and homespun blankets, and the men brought boxes of groceries. And so with all the gifts heaped upon the altar (the gold, the silver, the flowers, the candy and toys, the bread, the blankets and the groceries), the people of Charvel waited in the dark for the window to light up. But the window and the church remained as dark as ever. The people were confused and angry. They thought they had been tricked into giving. People were about to leave,

when suddenly, the woman outside—unknown to
the men guarding the door—silently made her way
down the aisle.

The Woman crosses her right hand and arm under her left
elbow. Thumb under her chin. Curled first digit. Rubs her upper lip.
Hears the silence.

> She knelt at the altar, prayed, rose, took her shawl
> and placed it inside out reverently upon the altar,
> beside the other gifts. The reversed shawl revealed
> an exquisitely embroidered picture of a man and a
> woman standing beside a well. They were sharing
> a cup. They were speaking with one another.
> Suddenly, as if a match had lit a very large candle, a
> burst of beautiful light streamed from the window.
> And the whole church lit up as bright as noonday.

Darkness has crept into the Woman's hotel room. She reaches
over. To the bedside table. Turns on the lamp. Thinks about the
gospel woman of Samaria. As a woman of Sa Maria. How she
went to her neighbours, saying. "Come and see a man who told me
everything I have ever done!"[28] Wonders again if Sa Maria is a clue.
A key unlocking the mystery that bars the door. Keeps. Darkness.
Light. Creeping in. A verbal coincidence. That editors had let creep
in. To help poor illiterate people know that Maria is the mother of
God, the sacred heart. The wellspring of their Christian story.

> The stranger, thought to be a woman of ill renown,
> too poor and too sinful to have a worthy gift, turned
> out to be a woman with a very extraordinary gift. So
> illuminating and holy was her gift that the church
> community of Charvel placed her name right
> beside Antoine's on the memorial plate beneath the

window. From that day on the window gleamed in the sunlight and glowed in the candlelight, and everyone's gift was declared worthy. And from then on no one was ever excluded or exiled from the communion of Charvel.[29]

The next morning, outside the colossal tent. The air is cool. The Woman shivers. Wanting to be a picture. An icon. Standing. With her shawl folded over one shoulder. Waits for the Greek.

She sees several people she recognizes: Mercy Oduyoye, the Methodist from Africa who spoke at the Lutheran Centre Well in Vancouver; Father Jeremiah, the Roman Catholic priest she sat with on the shuttle bus from Sydney; Lois Wilson, the first female moderator of the United Church of Canada; Marion Best, the United Church delegate from BC. They hurry by.

The Woman checks her watch. The one her 12-year-old daughter gave her. A Timex. Suntan brown leather strap. Starry night, moon phase. Cut out on the face. It's almost time for worship.

Around the corner. The Greek comes. He's wrapped in a shawl. A camel-colour pashmina with fringe. He kisses her on both cheeks. Like Greeks do. Motions for them to sit on the chairs. He positions himself facing her. The bold and white tent. Sitting on the lawn. Near the copse of willows. More people file past.

The Greek looks directly into the Woman's eyes. His eyes, full of sleepy desire, are tender and loving.

She reaches over. Remembers the Gospel story of the woman with the issue of blood,[30] and the day in mid-January when the Persian Gulf War escalated.

Mid-January 1991.

The Woman was in her gynaecologist's office with an issue of blood. She had come often. The doctor came into the waiting room and ushered her into his staff room to watch the television news bulletin. Concerned for her. He was a Christian, well established in a wealthy congregation in Vancouver. He knows she had been chosen as one of 10 accredited Canadian visitors to the 7th Assembly of the WCC in Canberra. He thinks it might be called off. Being too dangerous for delegates and visitors to travel. After the broadcast. They talk about the Woman's haemorrhaging.

"You'll be forty next month. It's been 12 years since I delivered your daughter. Since your tubal ligation. You're haemorrhaging, bleeding for three and four weeks with one week between cycles. It's your body's way of saying it's under stress and malnourished. You can stay home, eat more and exercise less. Stop playing in the big league."

Looks at the Woman. Sees her spunk. Says: " Something tells me you're not going to do that. You're hoping he'll be there. You'll touch the hem of his robe and be healed."

A month later.

Outside the tent. Touching the Greek's pashmina. As the Woman remembers. She marvels at the coincidence. Who would have thought? That the Greek would give her this opportunity to "touch" him as Jesus did in the Bible. How could he know she was haemorrhaging? She blushes.

Could he smell her blood? Did he smell her outside the World Vision booth? Did she smell? Or did someone known to him see him kiss her on both cheeks? Then see her go to the Assembly physician? His office, a curtained room, tucked away in the media room. The room for the press.

The Greek watches. The Woman's short-cropped auburn hair drift about her face. With the soft morning breeze. The hot Australian sun kisses her hair. Tans her alabaster skin. Studies her Wedgwood diamond patterned shawl. Tells her she is even more beautiful.

The Woman knows now. It is not over. Left alone with him. She would love him. Lie down and uncover his feet. His love and desire for her is too strong. She feels it. Wants him. To feel loved. Valued for her faith. That dares to touch. His robe.

He lifts his Assembly bag to his knee. It's different from the Woman's. It's plain unbleached cotton with an etched red pen-and-ink drawing of a dove. Wings resembling flames.

He looks inside. Finds a two-fold piece of paper. Hands it to her.

On the cover page of an article is a pen-and-ink drawing of a woman and a man tied back to back. Below are the words

"Face to Face"
Literature and Art
in the Renewal of The Church's Mission.
A Project
of the Orthodox Academy of Crete

The Greek gives her a moment. To take this in. Inside there is the invitation the Greek himself has presented to artists, painters, sculptors, carvers, poets and composers from all over the world.

He tells her. Write something. A story. A play. On the project theme: Macarios' dialogue. I can then invite you to come to Greece. Present you as the author.

The Woman looks at him. His eyes are serious. Full of love—the mysterious, tangled web is there.

How can I go to Greece? Ask my husband to come and see … a man who's seen me naked? Who loves me. Author something to make peace and reconciliation. With him and his wife. I'm a homemaker. No money of my very own. Mother. United Church Presbyterial president. Rich in faith. No modern worthy talent.

She sighs.

The Greek, seeing a colleague, excuses himself. The Woman, invitation safely in her bag, rises, makes her way to the tent. Strains of "Santo, Santo, Santo. *Mi Corazon te adora*" come out of the flaps.

60

Six

Linda Vogt Turner

Day 10
Canberra
February 16, 1991
Colossal white tent, after the Eucharist.

The Woman sits by the door of the tent. Waits for worshippers and communicants to clear. Bible study participants to assemble. Fishes in her cotton blue jean bag. For the Academy of Crete project article. Reads:

> Abba Macarios said that, while walking in the desert, he found the skull of a dead man on the ground: "As I moved it with my palm stick, the skull spoke. And I asked: 'Who are you?'
>
> "The skull responded: 'I was a high priest serving the pagans who had remained in this area. You are Macarios, the spirit-bringer. Every time you show your compassion to the damned and pray for them, they feel some consolation.'
>
> "The Saint asked him: 'What sort of consolation is this, and how is hell?'
>
> "The skull answered: 'The fire under us is as great as the distance between the sky and the earth; we stay in the middle of the fire from our feet to our head. And it is impossible to see each other face to face, because everybody is tied back to back to the other. Whenever you pray for us, we can partially see the face of the other. This is the consolation.'"[31]

The Bible study gets underway. The Woman puts the dialogue away. Gets the study booklet out. Listens. The Keynote introduces. The theme: the Lukewarm Angel of Laodicea. The Keynote stresses how the angel is neither cold nor hot. Because the angel has no desire, no need for anything. The speaker draws an analogy using the rich people of the world. Says they do not realize they are spiritually poor. That they need to repent and turn to God.

The Woman rubs her finger over her lips.

When it is time to discuss this in small groups, the Keynote suggests people pull their chairs together to form a circle of five or six. Choose a moderator. Accept a volunteer.

It's her turn to speak. "I think the Keynote has missed the point. This scripture is from the book of Revelation. It's a well-known fact that people have lost the key to understanding this book. Nothing is the secret. The lost wisdom. The lukewarm angel knows this. He's a stoic philosopher."

Someone cuts the Woman off. Reiterates what the Keynote has said.

The Woman is unable to say her next thoughts. *The true witness and the origin of God's creation is the great nothing ... the very womb of life. It is this womb of life that spits him out. Gives birth to him. Reproves him. Blesses him with life.*

The small group leader thanks both of them for their contribution. Wants everyone to feel included. Have a turn speaking to the text. Asks the next person in the circle. To comment. The next person also agrees with the Keynote.

At that moment the Greek appears. At the door of the tent. He remains stoic. Neither hot nor cold. Says nothing. Waits for the Woman to notice him. Her back is to the door. A strange silence falls over the group. She turns. Stands. Walks toward him. Leaves her bag. The scripture passage of the rich ruler pops into her head: *"Good teacher. What must I do to inherit eternal life?"*

The Woman. No money of her own, thinks herself rich. She has the choice to stay at home with her children. To volunteer and preside over 200 women. Knows. The Greek is the good teacher. Recognized here with her.

A [person] ran up and knelt before him, and asked him, "Good Teacher, what must I do to inherit eternal life?" Jesus said to [her], "Why do you call me good? No one is good except God alone. You know the commandments: 'You shall not murder; You shall not commit adultery; You shall not steal; You shall not bear false witness; You shall not defraud; Honor your father and mother.' "[She] said to him, "Teacher, I have kept all these since my youth." Jesus, looking at [her], loved [her] and said, "You lack one thing; go, sell what you own, and give the money to the poor; and you will have treasure in heaven; then come follow me." When [she] heard this, [she] was shocked and went away grieving, for [she] had many possessions.[32]

The Greek learned to watch people as a boy. Pay attention to things people deliberately say and do—read between the lines.

Saw the Woman leave her bag.

Deliberately.

Without a word. The Greek leads her off. To the tables outside. Near the World Vision booth. At a place selling coffee.

She tells him she has left her bag behind. She has no money. He will have to pay for her.

At the table. She doesn't ask him about the Eucharist. Her disobedience. Deliberate defiance of the Patriarch's High Priest. Doesn't ask: "Why didn't you stop me? Were you trying to placate me? Keep me quiet. Lest people find out. That we committed adultery the moment we met. When you looked at me and loved me. And I looked back."

He says: "Well, what do we need to talk about?"

She says: "You start. Ask me a question."

He asks: "What were you discussing? In the tent. The Bible study. Just now."

"The angel of Laodicea. The Keynote criticized the angel for being lukewarm, neither hot nor cold. I disagreed."

"Good.... Why?"

"I said I thought the Keynote had missed the point. This scripture is from the book of Revelation. It's a well-known fact that people have lost the key to understanding this book. Nothing is the secret. The lost wisdom. The lukewarm angel knows this. He's a stoic philosopher."

"Good." The Greek reaches into his breast pocket. Fishes out a cigarette. A match. Lights it.

The Woman asks: "Did you get my letters?"

"Yes."

"Did you read them?"

"Yes."

"Why didn't you write back?"

"I travel all the time. I live a terrible life of airports. I can't read or write in English. I gave your letters to my students to read. They highlighted them and summed up the important points."

"What do you think?"

"Of your work? It's not my place ... to critique your work." The Greek pulls hard on the cigarette, taking a long drag. Blows smoke away from her—pushing out his bottom lip.

She plays with her earring. Pushes the stud back and forth on the post. Not satisfied with the Greek's answer, she says: "I'm not an academic. I'm not ordained. I don't even have a university education. *Your opinion matters.* What do you think? Of my work. My writing."

"It's rich."

The Woman questions his response with her face. Her eyes.

Silence

"Let me tell you a story.

"The richest man in Greece was very rich. A colleague came to him one day and said, 'You are the richest man in all Greece. And you can neither read nor write in English. Just think. Where would you be if you could?' The rich man replied, 'I would be a poor monk in an obscure monastery.'"

The Woman smiles. Their shared experience at the assemblies makes them rich. Because he has not written to her, her faith has increased. She's had to figure things out for herself. Had she studied theology in a seminary, she would be a poor nun. In an obscure monastery. Not here talking with him.

The Woman sighs. Rubs her lips with the first digit of her left hand. The Woman says to the Greek: "It's about credibility. Without ordination, women have less credibility. Churches won't send women as delegates to conferences such as this. Some churches only have one seat. So they choose the highest-ranking ordained male. Without education and without ordination, women's voices are stifled."

She is well aware of the issues that divide their two faith traditions. Women such as Lois Wilson, Mercy Oduyoye and Chung Hyun Kyung are calling for the education and ordination of women. Are adamant that the churches include women in the politics and decision-making of the Ecumenical church.

Just the other day Lois Wilson stood up in the plenary, in her capacity as a former moderator of the United Church of Canada and one of the seven presidents of the WCC, and reproached the delegates, saying: "If Jesus were here today, He would say the politics of this assembly stink to high heaven."

Two male delegates appear at the table. They are friends of the Greek. They say: "Who is this? Introduce us."

They're Lutheran. German delegates. Aware of the programme schedule. The cancellation of the debate between the Greek and Professor Chung Hyun Kyung.

One German says to the Woman: "So what do you say? Is the Holy Spirit male or female?"

Her face and eyes sparkle. Mouth reveals an ivory grin. She says: "Female. And you?"

"We can see for ourselves that She is female."

The Woman is not sure. What the Germans mean. Do they think she is She, the Holy Spirit who has come to proclaim the second coming? She would like to believe that. As incredible as that would sound to people. Believing in the omnipotence and omnipresence of God. How could an ordinary, imperfect homemaker embody God and make such a proclamation? She'd be mocked and ridiculed. Declared crazy. Demon possessed. Like the Magdalene.

The Woman turns to the Greek. "And you?"

His perfectly controlled body reveals no emotion. "The Holy Spirit is Jesus."

The Woman calmly watches him. *What are you saying? My letters are filled with the idea that the Holy Spirit is the Magdalene, the female Jesus. Did your students highlight those passages? Did you read them?*

The Woman wonders. *Does he accept that patriarchal language and culture portray the Holy Spirit as He?* Her intuition tells her it's up to the disciples to figure this out. To discern the mystery. To receive the Holy Spirit as the She, the one who comes in His name, in the name of the Father and the Son. The third person in the Trinity.

The Germans accept all that has been said at the table. They leave.

The Greek lights another cigarette. The Woman takes a sip of coffee. Says: "I'm going to be 40 on Monday."

Exhaling. The Greek says: "Forty is significant. We must celebrate. Go out to dinner."

"I'd like that."

"Good. It's a date. Now. We must go. Back to our groups."

Back at her group.

The Woman collects her things. Takes her seat. The group is lukewarm. It's as if she has never left. They break for lunch.

The Woman finds a food booth that sells spring rolls. There, a Buddhist monk invites her to walk with him.

They walk toward the fountain in the centre of the square outside the plenary hall. Where the delegates assembled for the justice and peace march out to the tent. For an evening vigil. Last week. The children led the way. Australian Aboriginal people thought they

were supposed to lead. Canadian and American Indigenous people
stepped aside. In solidarity. Sang "We Shall Overcome."

Later. In the Tent. At the vigil. The white female organizer, with
an Australian accent, apologized. Asked for forgiveness.

The Monk. Shaved head. Dressed in a long maroon outer robe
over a saffron inner garment. Walks alongside the Woman. Clad
in her shirtwaist, short-sleeved desert dress. Bare legs. Loafers. Her
ID tag clearly visible. The Woman naïvely thinks she is invisible.
Unworthy of media attention. She's already forgotten the Eucharist,
the TV camera in her face. The cancelled debate between the Greek
and Professor Hyun Kyung. The conversation with the Germans
and the Greek. Doesn't think it curious that a brightly clad monk
should want to spend the lunchtime break with the Woman causing
the morning's uproar.

"Where are you from?"

"Vancouver, Canada. Delta actually. A suburb."

"So that's why you like Asian food. Lots of Chinese and Koreans
there.

"Yes, and you, where are you from?"

"Pusan, South Korea."

As they walk, the Monk tells the Woman that Pusan was a
refugee camp during the Korean War. It has a climate similar to
Vancouver. When it snows, people don't know how to drive. The
Woman laughs. Then her eyes dim.

Wonders. *Should I apologize? Ask for forgiveness? For taking up the
time. Set aside for the debate between the Greek and the Korean woman.
How can I? I don't have an official voice, merely an accredited visitor.*

The hall is the Australian Convention Centre. Concrete and steel
architecture. Outside. A covered porch. Stairs leading to a square.
A fountain. Reminds the Woman of Simon Fraser University. In
Vancouver. A place of Vietnam War and civil rights protests. Where
she went to smoke and study for her high school finals. Where she
planned to study, before she met her husband.

The plenary hall has high ceilings. Floor to ceiling windows. No air conditioning. Everyone has an accordion-folded paper fan with a red tassel. Open. A semicircle. Displays the 7th Assembly logo. Red. Cross in boat. Not blue. Like the banners.

The Woman and the Monk sit on the concrete edge of the fountain. Its mist and the trees nearby cool them. Face-to-face. Christian and pagan. The Woman tells the Monk the story of the woman from Samaria, how a Samaritan Jew had a theological conversation with an Orthodox Jew, even though it was forbidden. The Orthodox promised the Samaritan an eternal fountain an indwelling eternal life giving spring. For her trust and faith in him and their father.

The Monk then says: "Let me tell you a Buddhist story. It goes like this:

> Two monks, going to a nearby monastery, walk in silence side by side. When they come to a river they need to cross, they notice the water is higher than usual and that a young woman is there waving to them. She's reluctant to cross because of the high water and asks them to help her.
>
> The younger monk takes his vow of chastity very seriously and tells the woman that he can't help her.
>
> The woman replies with a little smile, "Nothing I ask will cause you to break your vow. I simply need help across the river."
>
> Blushing, the young monk replies: "I … I can't help you."
>
> "No worries," says the older monk. "I'll help you. Climb on my back."
>
> When the threesome reach the other side, the older monk puts the young woman down, and she thanks him with a big smile.

The two monks then continue on their way to the nearby monastery in silence.

Breaking the silence, the young monk rebukes the older one, saying, "You broke your vow of chastity by carrying that young woman on your back."

The older monk replies: "She needed help, and when we got safely to the other side, I put her down. You didn't carry her or offer to help me. So why is she still on your back?"[33]

The Woman dips her hand in the fountain. Gives the Monk a big smile. "Both stories liberate people from the bondage of vows. Liberate people to act compassionately and with love."

They laugh. Talk some more. He invites her to his talk. Scheduled for later that day. "You'll see. There are many similarities between Christianity and Buddhism."

The Monk's talk. A small lecture hall. Theatre seats.

The Monk says: "We have five thou-shall-nots. Christians have ten. We Buddhists think of these five rules as a raft. We need this raft to get safely to the wilderness on the other side of the river. Similarly, you Christians need your rules to get you to the other side of your river ... the Jordan. Once safe on the other side, you have a dilemma. What should you do with your raft? If you discard it, how can others cross over? Similarly, if you take it with you, how can others cross over? And it is cumbersome. An impediment. You can't wander freely in the wilderness. Carrying it. What do you do?"

The Monk asks the participants to turn to their neighbours. Behind and beside. To discuss this question.

The Woman eagerly joins in. She thinks a rope or vine attached to a tree on the other side might help. Her neighbour behind her points out that a rope or vine is not featured in the story. Her neighbour beside suggests offering one's raft and self as a servant, to ferry people back and forth.

The Woman likes this idea. Adds: "People could take turns being the servant. Or they could wait for others to cross over. Lash rafts together. Form a bridge."

Sunday, February 17

The Woman worships with a Uniting Church of Australia congregation. The church sits on a corner. Its white steeple reaches into the sunny sky. Fortress-like doors open. To the prosperous neighbourhood. Brick homes, paved streets, sidewalks, lawns, flowers, shrubs. Cars. Buses.

After worship.

The minister invites the Woman to the manse for lunch. His wife and other worshippers are there. The Woman doesn't talk about the Assembly. People don't ask. They ask about. Abortion. Divorce. Homosexuality. Ordination. Working moms. The Woman feels safe here. Tells them that she is from the United Church of Canada. A liberal progressive thinking congregation. Like theirs. Her women's group fundraised to pay for her airfare.

She says: "I'm fortunate. I have the choice. To stay out of the paid workforce. To volunteer. Choice. Is what I'm about."

Someone asks the Woman to comment on the Ordination and Gay issue. "In my opinion, governing one's own body as a Christ-centered person qualifies one ... to accept the call for ordination regardless of sexual orientation."

The manse delegation likes her. Smile and nod. Tease her about her accent. Laugh at the way she says "out and about." Ask her to say it again. Raucously hoot and howl when she says: "Again?"

Monday, February 18

Her birthday finally arrives. The Woman meets Hector on the way to the plenary after worship. Tells him she's 40 today. That she and the Greek are going to celebrate. Have dinner.

Inside the plenary. They separate. The Woman wants to mingle. Hector heads to the security gate. Tables. Flank each side of the entrance. With reports and headsets. The guard checks his ID tag. Hector picks up the day's reports. A headset. Takes his place. Near the front. At one of the many tables reserved for official delegates. The balcony. Press. Advisors. Translators.

The place for the VIP wives and official advisors is behind the tables. On the floor. Three rows of chairs. At the back. On both sides of the centre aisle. The seats on the aisle have a clear view of the moderator's table. The microphones.

In the lobby. Before the security gate.

The Woman heads to a book display. On a glass table. By the window. Sees Mercy Oduyoye in her lively printed dress and matching head scarf. The Woman is dressed in a loose-fitting turquoise-green T-shirt. Tucked into a stone-washed denim, knee-length full skirt. Wedgwood diamond scarf over one shoulder.

Walks over. Smiles. Mercy smiles back. Eyes catch how the turquoise green brings out the Woman's eyes. The pinstripes at the bottom of the Woman's scarf.

The Woman picks up a thin, parrot-green book. Its cover says

Mercy Oduyoye

Who
Will Roll
the Stone
Away?

---

*The Ecumenical Decade of the
Churches in
Solidarity with Women*

Inside. The Woman notices the decade officially began at Easter in 1988. Doesn't notice that Mercy personally autographed the Woman's copy and dated it "at Canberra 1999." Maybe it was merely a mistake. Maybe not. The Woman is simply pleased. Mercy signed it.

On the back of Mercy's book, the Woman reads: "Mercy Oduyoye is one of the three deputy general secretaries of the World Council of Churches and the moderator of the Education and Renewal Unit."[34]

Eager to read more. The Woman heads to the security gate. Picks up the reports. Headset. Takes a seat. At the back. On the aisle.… A man walks by … a waft of cologne anoints her. It's the Greek's scent … she looks up. It's not him.

She opens Mercy's book. "This book is being written as we are preparing for the seventh assembly of the World Council of Churches.… The assembly theme 'Come, Holy Spirit—Renew the Whole Creation' has released an abundance of energy, especially as we pursue the concerns of the decade."[35]

Puts the book down. Looks around her. Sees male energy. Smells his scent. Lingering. Feels the hair. On her body stand up. Her heart beating. Turns the book over again, more alert: "Those responsible for the WCC in Geneva and here at the assembly not only want to increase the number of women participating in the assembly … they want to lift up women's voices and decade concerns at the assembly."[36]

The Woman turns around. Looks for Simeonca and Josephine. Others she has met. On the other side of security. In the washroom. Thinks.

That's where female energy is. Unspoken politics, bridge-making actions, smiles, hugs, kind words, help. Like the other day. An African woman showed me how to tie my scarf like hers. The cotton was too thick. It looked so silly on my head, we all laughed.

Smiling, the Woman adjusts her headset. Continues reading: "According to Mercy, the assembly theme calls the church to renew their spirituality and support theology that redeems both women and men. Pointing the finger of blame for the plight of creation is not helpful. We, the human race, are responsible and we the church pray for the Holy Spirit to renew us and the whole creation."[37]

What a wonderful day. I'm 40! The new heaven and new earth. Is not just a vain prophecy. A cloud of witnesses. Angels of mercy are working, watching, waiting to renew all. To lift those who wait … on eagle's wings.[38]

Mercy's words bounce. Inside the Woman. Reverberate. "I remember the time in my own life when I came to use the word solidarity from my innermost being."[39]

"Solidarity is when others, friends and people you never even dreamed were aware of you … make a personal connection with you … to let you know that they are 'on the same wave length' … that they are praying for you … giving you signs of encouragement and taking 'courage from your stand.'"[40]

The Woman sighs. Sits taller.

Yes! The Eucharist. Is solidarity in Christ. It says. We take courage from your stand. We have a personal relationship with Christ. We know. Christ's name. Christ's blood nourishes us. We are Christ's body. Created in God's image and eternal likeness, male and female. The Stone has rolled away. "[L]ove is as strong as death…it burns like blazing fire…"[41]

It's afternoon teatime. The Woman walks. Renewed. Confident. Out onto the portico. The refreshment table with the cold drinks is on her left. Hector on her right. They spot the Greek.

Hector blurts out. Loudly. "It's her birthday. You're celebrating."

The Greek looks at Hector as if Hector has just stepped onto the stage of a Greek tragedy. Foretelling the sack of Troy. Paris' death.

The Greek turns. Looks at the Woman. Her sparkling eyes. They see his alarm.

"I can't meet … keep our date tonight. I've got to rework the committee's resolution. Over dinner. Wait here. I'll be back in a moment."

He descends the stairs. Disappears into the horde taking refreshment around the misting fountain and shading trees. In the square.

Hector clenches his right fist. Shakes it. Says: "It's your 40th. birthday!"

Puts his fist down. Crosses his arms. Sighs. "You deserve a night out.… Come out with me. Protest the upcoming 500-year celebration of Columbus and the new world.

The Woman fixes her eyes on the scene below. What has happened? Did she betray the Greek? Get him in trouble? By confiding in Hector?

She looks at Hector. *Have I deceived myself? Has Hector been setting me up? To show me what a fool I've been. Chasing after the Greek.*

Looks down at the fountain.

I'm to blame. I confessed my adultery My desire to have a relationship with the Greek. Hector saw my tears. Read my poems. Why can't he see? I'm the Magdalene and the Greek's the Rabboni.

The Woman turns her eyes and her attention back to Hector. He's wearing a loose white shirt. The kind Hispanic men wear to weddings—with pleats. Embroidered flowers.

Hector doesn't realize. I didn't either. He's just outed the Greek. The Church is in a war. The Greek knows how to fight, play both sides undercover.

"Where is the celebration?"

"Not far from here. With the Spanish contingent. There's to be food … and a film."

The Woman agrees. They work out details. See the Greek return.

The portico is empty. The Greek goes and stands on the far side. Hector and the Woman are standing beside the refreshment table. The white linen cloth whispers in the wind. The Greek catches her eye. Deliberately turns his back. On them.

Hector says: "He wants you to go over there. Go."

Turning her back on the Greek, the Woman says to Hector: "No. Let me know if he comes this way … or leaves."

The three of them stand there. Hector watches. Does not understand this back-to-back standoff. The tension. Visible. In their bodies. Far from the crowd and the fountain. Below.

The Woman turns her head slightly. Sees pain in the muscles of the Greek's body. Feels the ropes of politics tightening their grip around the Greek and herself. Holding them back to back. The flames of mistrust about to consume them. Her heart screams with pain. She longs for the ropes to loosen. To be face to face with him. Reconciled. His people and hers.

The Woman stands her ground. This is her moment. To create a living tableau. Let her silence be heard. To protest. Politics and things that divide people. Keep them back to back. Bones and skulls. Hearts silenced.

She prays the right people see the Greek and her standing there. For what seems like an eternity. She hopes. The Greek understands. Her letters. This living tableau. Stares at the refreshment table. Watches water drip down the iced bowl of juice.

From somewhere a bell sounds. Time to return. People mount the steps. The Woman and Hector go inside.

Hector says: "Face it. You had a one-night stand. He got what he wanted. He doesn't want to have anything more to do with you.... That day I saw you weeping when the Greek went off with that girl, I knew."

Trembling. The Woman shows her ID tag to the security guard. Returns to her seat.

Hector's words "I knew" pierce the Woman's side. Exhaust her. She tries to catch her breath. Revive herself.

She looks around for Simeonca and Josephine. Their seats are empty. She puts on her headset. Adjusts the volume. Listens. To a translator's voice. He's translating a Greek speaker who has gone to the mike. Maybe it's the Greek. She's not sure. Can't see the speaker. Too many people are milling about. She missed the introduction.

The voice says: "You people in the West think that because you are modern, you have all the answers. You think we Greeks are old-fashioned. That we and the patriarchy are keeping the Church from progressing. Christianity is patriarchal. Greek patriarchy is nothing like Roman patriarchy. Roman patriarchy is what robbed women of their equality. Not Greek patriarchy. We Greeks were the first to receive Christ. We understand patriarchal language. We don't have to change him to her. We understand mystery. The language of God. We have the key. You've lost the key. You do not even know how important the Stoic philosopher is to Paul. Without Paul's faith in the Stoic philosophers whom Paul spoke with, the Gospel would never have been born."

The Woman grins, puts her headset down. *The Greek has listened to her. He has used her interpretation of the lukewarm angel to rebuke the plenary.*

Outside in the square. The Woman waits for Hector. Not on the porch. By one of the large glass doors at the side, letting people spill out, freely.

A local man from Saturday's Bible study comes up to her. Says: "Did you hear that?"

"Yes I did."

"What do you make of it?"

"It's what I said in the tent. I think the speaker knew this and got my point across very well. The Stoic philosopher is important to Paul. And so is faith. Without Paul's faith and understanding of patriarchal language and philosophic culture, Christianity would not have spread."

The local man says: "Paul's teaching is chauvinist."

"Many feminists slander and dismiss Paul as being irrelevant. They're not listening to Paul in the cultural context of the day. Paul stood up to the philosophers and was not afraid to oppose them."

"But Paul's teaching on marriage places women under male authority."

"Paul believed that women needed the protection of marriage.[42] Not because Paul was a chauvinist. Rather because Paul saw how Greeks and polygamy, not to mention the sacred profession of prostitution, were negatively affecting women.[43] In Paul's first letter to the Corinthians, Paul says a woman should have her own authority and neither the woman nor the man is independent of the other. Because both as do all things originate from God.[44]

The local man gives her a hug. Kisses her on the cheek. Tips his hat. Says g'day. Goes.

The Woman is left with her thoughts. *Am I merely a token, for the Greeks and their sympathizers to hold up as an outdated example of a woman of faith? Have I deluded myself? Let my imagination distort reality?*

Hector makes his way through the glass doors. "The Greeks *are* holding everyone back. They just don't get it. If they really were for unity, the Greek would never have turned his back on you like he did."

"The Greek gave me an opportunity this afternoon. To make a statement."

"Yeah sure. You're fooling yourself."

The Woman tells Hector about the dialogue of Saint Macarios. It's too much. He can't listen.

At the celebration. Hector and the Woman arrive in time for the introduction to the film. There is no translator. Everything is in Spanish. The Woman took Spanish in high school. She understands *un poquito.* She watches. The action tells her what's going on.

The film depicts a wedding, a celebration. The whole village takes part. And then as the viewers watch the wedding and get ready to take part in the joy of the villagers, the bride comes into view. Not as the viewers expect. The bride with flowers in her hair and covering her dress is lying in a box. The villagers lower her into a prepared grave.

After the film, the Woman and Hector discuss this image.

"Tell me. Was this film making a statement about how Christianity came and brought Roman Catholicism to the Americas ... burying Indigenous faith and culture in the process?"

"Yes. So tell me. Why can't you see? The Orthodox and the Roman Catholic patriarchal traditions are still doing it. They're oppressing women and people of colour."

"I disagree. Patriarchy is not the only enemy. People just need to open their eyes, their hearts, learn about forgiveness. Death does not conquer the Bride. She rises and proclaims the Resurrection."

"Mmm … if that were so, the Greek would have come over and spoken to you. Not left you and me standing there on the porch this afternoon."

The Woman has not shared her theological ideas or her faith fully with anyone except the Greek. She tries to share her ideas with people in her home church and Presbytery. When she does, people are not ready, not interested or afraid to listen, thinking she is crazy, demon-possessed. Others simply have their own agenda. They just can't see how a female Jesus can make a difference to the message of love your neighbour.

Feelings bombarding her like flames from an exploding bomb. The Woman leaves the 7th Assembly. Alone. Heads for Sydney to tour the city. To attend *The Mikado* playing at the Sydney Opera House.

The Woman hasn't found the bestseller in the church bookstore yet. Hasn't seen the bold parrot-green letters. Red circle. On a gold mat atop a red leafy cover. Stare up at her.

**IT WAS ON
FIRE WHEN I
LAY DOWN
ON IT**

○

**ROBERT
FULGHUM**

Show and tell—love is stronger than death.

Seven

An ice rink. There in the parking lot, a big box. Boasting the name Esquimalt's Archie Browning Sports Centre. There is a goliath hockey puck suspended on a pole, in front of the doors. Summoning people in summer leisure. It's the dry floor season. The cars drive up from the ferry. File in side by side. People spill out, greeting one another with hugs.

It's an annual conference, lively, expectant.

Esquimalt. In May.
The year is 2000.
The time is eight thirty.

The Woman is there. The one who met the Greek 17 years ago in Vancouver. She looks different. Hair cropped short. Coloured a rich brown. Tawny streaks gone. She's dressed like the others. Casual, sporty. Blue jeans, black turtleneck, white faux leather vest. Plastic clad name tag on a cord.

Inside. Polished concrete. Walls and ceiling white. Two menthol toothpaste-coloured swishes. One up. One down. Wrap two walls. Glass doors and windows. Upstairs. Downstairs. Connect inside with outside. Long tables. Chairs, black vinyl with chrome. Wait to be filled. On the right sits the stage, large projection screen, keyboard, drums, podium, black music stands and microphones. There could be tweed upholstered armchairs, beautiful banners and shrubs present. The Woman can't remember.

Alone. As she makes her way inside, lost in a lonely time. It's Mother's Day weekend.

Her thoughts take her back to her mother, to the hospital. Her mother says: "I sent Steve to get me a coffee, so I could tell you something. I know you don't want to hear this. Your dad and I were good partners. But we were not good lovers. We were like brother and sister, each wanting to outdo the other."

The Mother pauses. Looks into her daughter's starry blue eyes, as a nurse comes in.

"Mrs. Solly, sorry to interrupt. I need to check your signs, take your temperature." He checks the oxygen, the IV drip, listens to the Mother's chest with his stethoscope. Takes her pulse.

When he's gone, the Mother continues: "Had your dad not died, I would never have met Ernie and never known love."

"Why are you telling me this?"

"Steve is not your lover. He loves having you as a pretty wife, who dresses him up, gives him pretty children. But he feels trapped. Doesn't want to be the bad guy, dumping you, a churchgoer. He resents you. Your gregarious nature, your thirst for adventure, for knowledge, for theology. He doesn't share your passion. He doesn't want to do things with you, to get involved in the church. He doesn't even want to be here, visiting me."

It's too awkward.

"I'm dying."

In the vestibule, in front of the dry floor rink, glassed in. The Woman approaches the registration area. Moves to the desk. Gives her name to one of the sweatshirt-clad women sitting there. Buys a BC jade-green coffee mug. A gilded circle wraps sun, mountain wave swoosh ... sand footprints.

Moving through the glass doors separating the rink from the vestibule and concession area. The Woman's eyes connect with the projection screen and the words Displaced & Abundant, Conference 2000. Music may be beckoning her. "Come in, come in and sit down, you are a part of the family." She can't remember. She takes a seat at a table near the stage.

The Woman's thoughts take her back to her car, a little Colt. Somewhere on the freeway between Abbotsford and Delta. To the day she tried to tell her daughter about what Grandma Solly had said, before she died. Blurted out instead: "I'm going to ask your dad for a divorce."

This is too much for the girl. "You're just upset about Grandma. I don't believe you."

After the funeral, the Woman couldn't ask. She waited until after Christmas. At Easter, they began to ready the house for the market. Told the family, people close to them.

Seats near the Woman fill. Clergy, talented, articulate, church people draw her into conversation. Her confidence wanes. She a stay-at-home mom, a mature university student, about to be divorced after 30 years, has no status. Her demeanour changes. Body stiffens. Pulls back. She looks at the BC jade mug. The gilded circle. Gilded words: Displaced & Abundant sit above, Conference 2000 below.

Church teaching claims people matter even when they're displaced from their land, their position, their families or their health. People who matter are in God's covenant—the gilded circle. A decision to leave a dead marriage should not take one out of the gilded circle.

The next afternoon. A short stocky man, in beige sports slacks. Purple and gold wool pullover stands at the wall. Near her. His Scottish dun eyebrows, almond-brown eyes, take in the lie, carefully measuring the distance. He's a golfer. His complexion ruddy and outdoorsy. His drinker's nose, broad and flat. His wispy, thin hair, dun like his eyebrows. Greying at the temples. Boyish and priestly with a Friar Tuck bald spot.

She smells him. Her nostrils fill. Her lungs breathe in his strong, sophisticated, masculine scent. The scent of eternity. He takes a seat at her table. He knows George and Ella, an older couple. He's their minister. George politely introduces him to the Woman. Tells her he and Ella call him the Jazz Priest.

The Woman and the Jazz Priest chat. People at the table in front of them, turn and shush them.

He leans closer to the Woman. Whispers. "So what brings you here?"

The Woman places her slender, ring-less left hand on the table in front of her. "I'm the President of Fraser Presbyterial and a displaced person."

With his ring-less left hand, he places his cup on the table and whispers: "I'm a senior minister in Burrard Presbytery and displaced too."

The table groups deliberate on the resolution just presented. The Jazz Priest and the Woman use this to full advantage. They turn to face one another. Her blue eyes light up. Become electric. His almond-brown eyes hungry to know. Her deeply.

The Woman feels his power. Wants a connection. To his network. To the world church. To the Greek. She remembers. That day. She turned forty. She and the Greek standing back to back. On the portico. Facing the world church. Saint Macarios' dialogue. She carries it still in the blue jean cotton bag of her mind.

The words of Saint Macarios of Egypt are etched in her skull: "The fire under us is as great as the distance between the sky and the earth; we stay in the middle of the fire from our feet to our head. And it is impossible to see each other face to face, because everybody is tied back to back to the other."[45]

The Woman fishes for the right question. To entangle him. To loosen the ropes. To be face to face. With the other. The Greek. Her eternal quest.

She asks: "Have you ever been to Australia?"

"Yes. For a pulpit exchange."

"Did you attend the 7th Assembly of the World Council?"

"No. But I attended the pre-assembly event in San Antonio. Did you?"

"Yes. How come you didn't?"

"Busy with other things. I was on the national staff at the time on the Team of Evangelism. I could have gone. How about you? How did you get to go?"

"I attended the 6th Assembly as a daily visitor and wanted more. I applied for one of the ten accredited visitor positions and was accepted. I would have loved to have attended the 8th Assembly in Zimbabwe. But I was turned down. Others who had applied for Canberra were given priority. Have you travelled much?"

"Yes. On the national staff, I've been all over the world. Europe, the Middle East, Hong Kong, the Philippines, Australia. Never been to Cuba though. Just got back from Oberammergau. How about you?

"I went to Nicaragua in 1989 with GATE as part of a 10-person delegation to 'Gain Awareness through Experience.'"

Looking at her more closely. His golfer's eyes move from her face. To her sweater. Delicately ribbed body. How she sits. Relaxed. Casually playing with her earring. Her left thumb and first digit moving the butterfly up and down on its post.

His left thumb and left digit play with the heavy gold signet ring on the smallest digit on the right. The Jazz Priest says: "And did you? Gain awareness?"

She stops playing with her earring. "I had no idea people could be so cruel. Our tour guide was a young woman about 20. Attractive. She told us how she and her little brother helped their parents during the insurrection in '79. As children they would carry guns and information. The Contras got suspicious and wanted information about the whereabouts of their parents. So they took her and her little brother. They tortured her in front of her little brother. They pulled out her fingernails one by one. Her little brother did not talk. Neither did she."

She continues. "Another time, her father went missing. It was Christmas. For a present on Christmas Day, the Contras delivered the dead body of her father to her mother. They dumped him on the street in front of their house. Then before her mother could run out and kiss the body, they drove over the body. Back and forth. Back and forth. Until he was just a mangled mash of bloody pulp."

A voice from the stage says: "It's time to vote on the resolution."

Marion Best, the former moderator of the United Church of Canada, is there. She does not speak to the Woman. The Woman remembers Marion had been a delegate. At Canberra. Wonders if Marion saw her that day. On the portico. Recognizes her here, now.

Marion speaks for the resolution. To displace the formal BC Conference seat given to the President of the United Church Conference Women. Says that the UCW is aging. Presbyterials are no longer necessary. Women are participating fully in the life of the United Church of Canada as ordained and diaconal ministers. Men of faith serve their congregations and presbyteries. They have no auxiliary seat.

The Woman agrees with the women of her presbyterial. Opposes this resolution. Wants to speak against it. Can't. Knows she has to finish school. Get a job. No time to fulfill her duties in the coming conference year as Presbyterial Past President.

It's December 20.
The year is 2012.

The Woman doesn't want to remember. What comes after that day at the ice rink, the day she met the Jazz Priest. Today would have been their eighth wedding anniversary. It's dark. The Woman sits alone in an upstairs room, at a desk looking out. She can see lights in the street beyond the vacant townhouse lots that border her three-story house. She wants to shut out the memories of the Jazz Priest. His freshly shaved and scented face. The way he blew his nose. Working the tissue. Pushing his nose up and down. She doesn't want to remember all his funny little sayings, the silly little things they did together, the stupid quarrels, the hot steamy sex and the many places they did it.

Four years ago they were so happy. They went out to dinner somewhere to celebrate their fourth wedding anniversary. She can't remember where. This bothers the Woman. The Jazz Priest liked to eat out, to walk into a fine restaurant with her on his arm. Had she known he would die in Cuba the following month she would have paid more attention.

She returns to bed. Thinks. Remembers:

It is late June 2000.

The weather is warm and sunny. The Jazz Priest is waiting for her at the SkyTrain Station at Burrard in downtown Vancouver. He waves to her from the curb where he's parked his late-model car, a teal-blue Acura. Inside the car, the Woman focuses her attention on him as he drives. His masculine air, the smell of eternity, the leather seats, the wood paneling on the dash, the gentle breeze from the sunroof vie for her attention. He informs her of his plans. He's taking her to Rossini's. It's a jazz club.

Across the street is Kits Beach. There is a parking lot there. He parks and puts money in the machine. As they cross the wide expanse of grass that separates the lot from the edge of the road, the Woman asks: "How old are you?"

"Sixty-one next month. And you?"

"Forty-nine."

"Twelve years is not that much."

The Woman lowers her sea-blue eyes. Watches her feet make prints in the long grass. She doesn't want to think about the wide expanse. They get to the street. Wait at the light. Her eyes study his sturdy legs in oyster-shell trousers and shoes. Climb up to his belly, belted with brown leather and buttoned in summer blue and yellow stripes. Inch past those buttons on his belly. Linger on those at the collar. There. Inside. At his neck. A little gold Celtic cross.

The light changes. They cross the street and enter Rossini's. Inside, everything is alive with sound. The music draws the people, cutlery and crockery into communion. She feels it the moment she steps inside. The close feeling of connection that is this place.

She wakes to the sound of the telephone. Smiles. She knows who it is. The Singer. It makes her happy to wake to the sound of his voice. He tells her about how he sometimes falls asleep in the evening and then wakes up at one thirty or so in the morning. When this happens he writes. She says this too happens to her. It happened today. He knows she's writing a book about the Greek. She wants the Singer to understand. She loves his voice. He's the Singer who makes her sing.

She returns to her desk. Thinks about something he wrote and read to her the other day—how people who have loved us in the past, before our destruction or theirs, may wait for us in the future.

Slowly, an image comes to the Woman. Centuries ago, a woman came to Simon's house in a village called Bethany. She had an alabaster jar filled with a fragrant mixture.

The Jazz Priest drowned on the beach. In Cuba. It wasn't suicide. Nor was it merely an accident. It was his time. To return to eternity. To help her know. That she's lived before. That yet another waits like a young hart at the gate for her.[46] Another image flashes into her mind—Hart House in Deer Lake Park—the place where she and the Jazz Priest celebrated their fourth anniversary.

She wants the story of love safely contained, but that summer night almost 30 years ago, and again this morning in the upper room, is a mystery. Hears the words "Open to me my sister, my love, my dove, my undefiled."[47] Knows. She has to tell this story so others remember that love is stronger than death.

Additional Resources

Adams, Lawrence E. "The WCC at Canberra: Which Spirit?" First Things website, June 1991. http://www.firstthings.com/article/1991/06/005-the-wcc-at-canberra-which-spirit (accessed November 19, 2014).

Cloud, David. "The World Council of Churches (Part 2)" La Vie Éternelle website, March 7, 2014. http//la-vie-eternelle.blogspot.ca/2014/03/the-world-council-of-churches-part-2.html (accessed November 19, 2014).

Erlanger, Steven. "Women Challenge Church Council Assembly." *New York Times*, February 20, 1991. http://www.nytimes.com/1991/02/20/world/women-challenge-church-council-assembly.html (accessed November 19, 2014).

In Plain Site website. "World Council of Churches." http://www.inplainsite.org/html/world_council_of_churches.html (accessed November 19, 2014).

About the Author

Linda Vogt Turner is a lay writer and educator living in Metro Vancouver, Canada, where she was born and educated. Linda has written extensively on faith and justice themes. She completed her master of arts degree at Simon Fraser University (SFU) in 2011. The title of her master of arts thesis project is *Mary Magdalene: Her Image and Relationship to Jesus.* Full text is available online at http://summit.sfu.ca/item/12048.

Linda is a member of the United Church of Canada where she is a council member and lay presbytery delegate for Bethany-Newton United Church. She participated in the 6th Assembly of the World Council of Churches held in Vancouver during the summer of 1983.

In 1989, Linda travelled to Nicaragua. There she witnessed the poverty and political struggle of the Sandinista government as Nicaragua recovered from the 1979 insurrection and the continued guerrilla resistance of the Contras. Two years later, during the Gulf War, Linda participated in the 7th Assembly of the WCC in Canberra, Australia. Inspired and responding to the 7th Assembly call to "renew the whole creation," she returned home and enrolled in university to learn more about socio-economics, human systems, culture and politics.

Seventeen years later in June 2008, as an administrative assistant at SFU and a graduate student, Linda responded to the first ECOTHEE call for papers held at the Orthodox Academy of Crete (OAC) under the Auspices of the Ecumenical Patriarch to honour World Environment Day. Subsequently, Linda has been a co-organizer and moderator for the OAC-sponsored 2010 Conservation and Sustainable Use of Wild Plant Diversity conference, the ECOTHEE 2011, 2013 and 2015 conferences, and the 2012 and 2014 Sustainable Alternatives to Poverty and Eco-Justice conferences in Crete and Madagascar. In 2012 she chaired the Inter-Ecothee Green the Scene Symposium held at Bethany-Newton United Church.

The Ecumenical Affair is about Linda's love for the Gospel and her passion for Christian unity.

Endnotes

1   Maria-Teresa Porcile-Santiso, "Roman Catholic Teachings on Female Sexuality," in *Women, Religion And Sexuality*, ed. Jeanne Becher (Geneva: WCC Publications, 1990), 192–3.

2   Robert Fulghum, *It Was on Fire When I Lay down on It* (New York: Ivy Books, 1989), 170.

3   Ibid., 170.

4   Ibid., 173.

5   Ibid. 174-175.

6   Ibid., ix–xi.

7   Ibid., 3.

8   Ibid.

9   William H. Lazareth, *The Triune God: The Supreme Source of Life (Thoughts Inspired by Rublev's Icon of the Trinity)*. Document TH4-4 Vancouver BC: World Council of Churches Sixth Assembly, 1983, l.

10 Song of Solomon 5:2–5, 8:6 (New Revised Standard Version).

11 John 8:5 (NRSV).

12 Robert Fulghum, *It Was on Fire When I Lay down on It* (New York: Ivy Books, 1989), 3.

13 Ibid.

14 Harriet Ziegler. "Female View Important to Theology." *SHEKINAH* Double Issue, Vol. 4# 3&4, (July–December 1983), 17. the-branch.org/ Ordination_Of_Women_WCC_Shekinah_Magazine_Branch_Report (accessed October 23, 2014).

15 John 4:9 (NRSV).

16 John 4:10–14 (NRSV).

17 John 4:15–20 (NRSV).

18 John 4:21–26 (NRSV).

Linda Vogt Turner

19 Luke 8:17 (King James Version).
20 Revelation 21:16–17 (Revised Standard Version).
21 Genesis 26:12 (NRSV).
22 Numbers 21:9 (New American Standard Bible).
23 Galatians 3:28 (New International Version).
24 Philippians 2:10 (NRSV).
25 Luke 4:18 (NRSV).
26 John 4:26, 14 (NRSV).
27 Revelation 21:2, 3,6 (RSV).
28 John 4:29 (NRSV).
29 This story was adapted by the author. Another version can be found in Cheryl Perry's *Live the Story: Simple Short Plays for Churches*. Wood Lake, 1997.
30 "Now there was a woman who had been suffering from haemorrhages for 12 years; and though she had spent all she had on physicians, no one could cure her. She came up behind him and touched the fringe of his clothes, and immediately her haemorrhage stopped" (Luke 8:43–44 NRSV).
31 Orthodox Academy of Crete (*Apophthegmes Sancti Macarii Aegyptii* 38, PG 34:257C-258A. See also *Les apophthegmes des Pères, Sources Chrétiennes* 484 (Paris 1993), 158–60.)
32 Mark 10:17–22 (NRSV).
33 *Lotus: At the Heart of Symbolism.* "Crossing Over." users.skynet.be/lotus/story/story-en.htm (accessed October 27, 2014).
34 Mercy Oduyoye. *Who Will Roll the Stone Away?* (WCC Publications, Geneva, 1990) 7.
35 Ibid., 38.
36 Ibid., 38–9.
37 Ibid., 38–40.
38 Isaiah 40:31 (NRSV).
39 Mercy Oduyoye. *Who Will Roll the Stone Away?* (WCC Publications, Geneva, 1990) 43.
40 Ibid.
41 Song of Solomon 8:6 (NIV).
42 1 Corinthians 6:15–20, 7:1–2, 36–38 (NRSV).
43 John T. Bristow. *What Paul Really Said about Women* (Harper Collins Paperback, 1991), 111.
44 1 Corinthians 11:10–11 (NRSV).

45   *Apophthegmes Sancti Macarii Aegyptii* 38, PG 34:257C–258A. See also
     Les Apophthegmes des Pères, Sources Chrétiennes 484 (Paris 1993), 158–60.

46   Song of Solomon 8:14 (KJV).

47   Song of Solomon 5:2 (KJV).

Printed in the United States
By Bookmasters